OVERCOMING
ILLUSIONS ABOUT
BIOTECHNOLOGY

NICANOR PERLAS

Zed Books Ltd
London and New Jersey

Third World Network
Penang, Malaysia

Overcoming Illusions about Biotechnology
is published by Zed Books Ltd., 7 Cynthia
Street, London N1 9JF, UK and 165 First
Avenue, Atlantic Highlands, New Jersey
07716, USA, and by Third World Network,
228 Macalister Road, 10400 Penang, Malaysia.

Printed by Jutaprint, 54 Kajang Road,
10150 Penang, Malaysia

ISBN:1 85649 303 2 Hb
1 85649 304 0 Pb

A catalogue record for this book
is available from the British Library.
US CIP is available from
the Library of Congress.

CONTENTS

PART IV   Controlling the Biotechnology Revolution

PREFACE

This book has its origin in a lengthy paper presented in an international conference on 'Global Development and Environment – Has Man a Future?' The conference was held in Penang, Malaysia, in 1987 and was organized by the Asia Pacific Peoples Environment Network and Sahabat Alam Malaysia (SAM – Friends of the Earth Malaysia). The paper was then titled 'Development and Environment in the Age of Biology: Assessing and Controlling the Profound Impacts of Biotechnology on Nature, Human Beings, and Society'.

The use of the term 'profound impacts' may sound presumptuous especially in the light of recent industry propaganda calling for a relaxation of biosafety regulations. The benefits of genetic engineering continue to be heavily advertised and the risks too little discussed, so much so that, unknown to many, the dangers of biotechnology have already surfaced, as can be seen in the examples below:

● US scientists have transplanted the entire AIDS virus genome into laboratory mice. In February 1990 scientists reported the potential creation of a 'super AIDS' virus which was formed when the ordinary AIDS virus combined with native retroviruses in the mice. Worse, some scientists believe that this more virulent AIDS virus might be capable of being transmitted by air!

● L-tryptophan is a natural product sold for decades at health food stores. This compound is used to treat insomnia and depression. L-tryptophan was always considered safe for use by consumers. However, a Japanese firm started producing the product through biotechnology processes. And when the genetically engineered L-tryptophan reached consumers, dozens of users died and hundreds more were made seriously ill.

● Thousands of children in the US today use genetically engineered human growth hormone (HgH). However, these expensive drugs may be dangerous as they have been linked with leukaemia and melanoma.

The potential impacts of biotechnology are so profound and far-reaching that there is a need for a comprehensive assessment of biotechnology. This need is reinforced by the increasing number of international and national institutions which are starting to view biotechnology as their alternative to the pesticide-based 'green revolution' in agriculture that they once promoted but are now rejecting.

Unfortunately, no favourite perspective or existing paradigm can encompass the demand for a multidimensional assessment of biotechnology. In this book, I propose a new, integrative framework for assessing and dealing with the vast challenge of biotechnology.

The new framework builds upon social and environmental critiques of technology. However, the framework adds a new dimension for assessing biotechnology: the spiritual. The actual patenting of segments of the human genome can no longer be fundamentally addressed from a purely social or environmental perspective alone. Illuminating the problem of patenting of life raises the larger questions regarding the origin of life and the meaning of human existence.

The term 'spiritual' here is used in an unconventional way. To appreciate the usage of the word 'spiritual' requires thoughtful reading of the book. The reader is especially encouraged to read the section on the 'second scientific revolution' where it is shown how quantum physics and other scientific developments are increasingly affirming the reality of the spiritual.

The North and other industrializing countries may have dismissed the spiritual from its policy considerations. However, this is not the case in many developing countries. They are increasingly recognizing that the loss of a sense for the sacred has played a tremendous role in the breakdown of nations and the unrelenting destruction of nature.

Such an introductory effort must of necessity be incomplete. Furthermore, some readers may be immediately tempted to dismiss the framework as contradictory or simply impossible to achieve. I encourage readers to approach this work with an open mind. The book would have justified its existence if readers are exposed to a whole new way of viewing the phenomenon of biotechnology even if they ultimately do not agree with it.

Increasing sophistication in assessing the potential impacts of biotechnology has highlighted the importance of alternative approaches to it. Biotechnology tempts society with promises of miracle cures for human diseases and increased productivity in agriculture. Yet, if detailed analyses show these promises to be problematic at best and illusory at worst, what do critics of biotechnology have to offer society? The health and food needs of society must be met somehow.

That this is possible is one of the most exciting developments in recent years. Trials, for example, at the University of California have shown that rotational grazing management is a better economic and ecological alternative to the use of genetically engineered bovine growth hormone. Large-scale sustainable efforts in the Philippines are already showing that the stem borer can be controlled by ecological pest management techniques without resorting to the deployment of genetically engineered Bt rice plants.

The power of more sustainable alternatives to biotechnology can only be indicated here in the preface and in a more generic manner in the book. It is being addressed in a more detailed manner in my forthcoming book entitled *Ecological Alternatives to Agricultural Biotechnology*.

Meanwhile it is important to mention that the issue of alternatives has entered into the regulatory guidelines of the National Biosafety Committee of the Philippines. Biotechnology researchers are now required to discuss alternatives in all projects proposing genetic engineering experiments.

Because of rapid developments in the subject areas of the original paper, especially in sustainable agriculture and biotechnology, I deemed it necessary to edit and amplify portions of the paper in preparation for this book. Addenda have been added in chapters where developments have been extensive. This, for example, was done on the chapter on sustainable agriculture. I have also added an introductory chapter to highlight the importance and relevance of the central issues taken up in the original paper in relation to today's contemporary challenges.

It must be remembered, however, that the preface and the lengthy introductory chapter do not attempt to update all the data contained in the book. This especially refers to studies cited in the book. One could cite more recent ones. Instead I have focused on updating the important themes of the book, emphasizing their enduring relevance to the concerns of today.

Due to pressures of work commitments, there are no footnotes in the book. Nevertheless I can guarantee the authenticity of the citations and facts contained in the book. I had to make a choice between, a) further delays in bringing the book into publication complete with footnotes and, b) having the urgent message of the book immediately available to the increasing number of individuals, non-governmental organizations (NGOs), and peoples organizations who are asking hard questions about the possible impact of biotechnology on their lives. I am, however, willing to provide the proper citation for those readers who write to me through the publishers of this book.

I wish to thank the publishers of this book, especially Martin Khor of Third World Network, who hounded me with letters and personal reminders, until finally there was no other recourse than to have it finished.

Nicanor Perlas
June 1994

INTRODUCTION

Genetic engineering and the other modern biotechnologies are so revolutionary that its proponents, early on, immediately tried to link biotechnology with something historical and traditional, something like the use of bacteria and yeast in food and wine making. They also tried to link it with ancient farming practices, claiming that genetic engineering is in essence no different from ancient breeding techniques that have benefited humanity for thousands of years.

The uncritical observer did not see the contradiction between this assertion and the fierce battle biotechnologists waged to obtain patents on life and life processes. Without agreeing to patenting of life and for the sake of exposing a contradiction, one can make the following observation: How can one claim novelty as is implicit in any patent application while at the same time saying that biotechnology is no different from historical uses of microbes and plant and animal breeding?

In any event, the ploy of the biotechnologists worked. Even prominent seasoned activists and environmentalists were ensnared in the definitional trap. Without knowing the history or technical details of genetic engineering, these well-meaning critics of biotechnology appropriated the language of the genetic engineer. They did not know that 'biotechnology' was synonymous with genetic engineering in the early days of the technology.

Some of them even tried to outdo the genetic engineers in their game. They even tried to expand biotechnology to include modern agro-ecological approaches and indigenous agricultural practices. In the process they only added to the confusion of the newcomers and those who wanted to make an independent evaluation of the significance of genetic engineering for humanity.

Language or word games may appear innocuous. But in the hands of experts, they can become tools for misleading and even dismantling the critical mind.

This issue, first pointed out in the 1987 paper, remains valid and important until today.

∗ ∗ ∗ ∗ ∗

The central framework of this book remains not only relevant today but has become even more indispensable in addressing the profound revolution that biotechnology will force on nature and human societies. The book's central theme requires immediate large-scale recognition and implementation if we are not going to be passive dumping grounds of high-tech promises and products. The multiple dimensions of technological impact have to be recognized if we do not want to see more environmental disasters, economic poverty, and social diseases – all inflicted in the name of hi-biotech and progress.

The book lays out in detail three dimensions of technology: social, resource/environmental and ideological/moral. The meaning of each dimension is explained in detail below. A total, comprehensive, balanced, and integrated perspective and assessment of technology and its role in society is so important and essential that I would like to include the following considerations in addition to those already articulated in the book especially in Part I.

The Three Historical Critiques on Technology

Technology, in one form or another, has been with mankind since the beginning of time. But modern technology, as we know it today, first became dominant in modern civilization with the industrialization of England. Technological application powered industrialization. Thus technology was closely associated with economic development and progress.

Social Critique

Economic 'progress' however generated the socialist critique of capitalism. Among others, this critique focused on 'development for whom?' and the related question of 'technology for whom?' This paradigm centred itself on the social impacts of techno-logical application in the process of economic development. The concerns included unequal distribution of wealth, inequitable access to technology, unfair ownership of resources, and others. Technology, in itself, was not questioned – only who controlled it and how it was applied. There was a neglect of the environmental and resource impacts of technology. And, except for a few prescient but almost forgotten social philosophers of that time (19th century), the ideological/moral dimension of technology was not even recognized.

Environmental Critique

While capitalists, socialists, and communists struggled over the fate of nations, employing technology for their own ends and purposes, a new problem with technology surfaced. Industrialized economies had to face the spectre of resource depletion in the midst of both localized and global environmental destruction. The book, *Silent Spring*, triggered the emergence of the global environmental movement in the 1960s. As the Earth

Summit has shown, the environmental critique coming from citizens movements and NGOs has since found receptive ears at the highest levels of corporate and state governance. Few environmentalists, however, took up the structural issues raised by Marxists, socialists, church groups and other sectors of society. The vast majority of this group continued to view 'technology as neutral'. Only, technology has to be fine-tuned so as not to create too much environmental and resource 'noises'.

Scientific/Philosophical Critique

Meanwhile, as social and environmental problems continued to accelerate and increasingly claimed larger and larger segments of nature and countries, a new generation of critics of the established order increasingly became visible. They were dissatisfied with purely social or environmental paradigms. While not oblivious to the importance of social and environmental concerns, they focused their sights on the hidden worldview, the hidden values, the hidden politics incorporated in the technology itself. For these people, science and technology are not neutral. They have their own agenda. To meaningfully solve social and environmental problems, the hidden agenda of science and technology have to be unmasked. When so illumined, then and only then, so say the critics of science and technology, can true societal transformation and peace with nature be achieved.

One-Sided Critiques

It is therefore understandable that activists from these different streams of social criticism have a difficult time understanding and appreciating each other's viewpoint. Each speak a different language.

Those who argue 'technology as neutral' are normally blind to the 'ideological' dimension and social impacts of technology. Those who focus on 'technology for whom?' and argue 'technology for the poor' are understandably blind to the 'ideological' or hidden agenda of technology and have a slight aversion for the resource and environmental impacts of technology. Finally, those who are insistent on illuminating the inner worldview, values, politics, and agenda of technology are often naive, even as they are open, about the larger socio-political questions that, of necessity, accompany the diffusion of technology in society.

These three classic cognitive habits are one-sided, incomplete and dangerous. Already policy makers, scientists, and NGO activists in the environmental, sustainable agriculture, and social movements are being split along various combinations of the three dimensions of technology.

How can we concretely observe these tendencies in the activism of today?

Environmentalism Without Soul

A significant number of environmental activists implicitly support or are victimized by the paradigm which believes that 'technology is neutral'. Thus they understandably focus their attention on ensuring that technology is 'environmentally friendly' and does not have adverse impacts on the resource base of a community, country, or the global commons. They are satisfied when some form of environmental assessment is included in development programs and initiatives. Therefore, a significant number of environmental organizations with international clout are linking up with large corporations oblivious to the large scale social impacts of their 'environmentally friendly' technologies.

This paradigm has led to an interesting phenomenon, a contradiction unsolvable within the environmentalist perspective on technology. Today large scale organic farms are existing in the United States and Latin America. Such a development is definitely good for nature and the pockets of the large scale farmers themselves. However, these corporate organic farms are displacing thousands of family farmers in the United States and even larger numbers of peasants in Latin America. Because promoters of environmentally friendly farming technologies paid little or no attention to social dynamics beyond ecology and economics, they were impotent in stopping the adverse impacts of technology in society.

Furthermore, this myopic environmental focus often leads them to aberrations in social behaviour. One increasingly encounters the phenomenon of environmental NGOs promoting 'environmentally friendly biotechnology' as a technological fix for complex socially-generated agricultural problems. Furthermore, large northern environmental NGOs try to dominate and control southern NGOs in their eagerness to help solve conservation problems in the South.

Social Activism Without Spirit

The limits of the 'technology for whom?' approach are surfacing in current discussions related to intellectual property rights (IPR). Transnational corporations are trying to gain control over the biodiversity of the South through IPRs. W.C. Grace has obtained patents or monopoly rights over certain applications of neem. Activists have branded this and similar efforts as 'biopiracy' or 'intellectual piracy'.

As discussed below, this dangerous trend is starting to dominate trade and other agreements among nations. As a counter approach, some well-meaning social and environmental activists are trying to obtain IPRs for indigenous communities (IC). They believe that, by playing the same game as their adversaries, they will be able to protect the interests of indigenous communities. These proponents of IPRs for ICs, however, have not seen through to the ideological/moral dimension of IPR, a biotech-related social technology.

IPRs are a mode of organizing property and ownership relations which presume the acceptance of certain value and beliefs of the North. These include greed as an engine in economic development, egotistic and private appropriation of bodies of knowledge and technique created in the public domain, monetary compensation for creativity that is perceived to be socially beneficial, and control over nature.

These Northern values and beliefs embedded in the IPR approach are alien to indigenous communities. Indigenous people have a more respectful and spiritual relationship with nature. They value sharing of common property and not exclusion of others. They view and value harmonious human relationships, not greed, as the pillar of their economy. They freely share their knowledge with others.

Thus well-intentioned activists who try to bring ICs into the IPR regime are, in effect, sowing the seeds of disharmony and dissolution of indigenous communities. Thus, in the end, it does not matter if those who assert a 'technology for whom?' paradigm have succeeded in 'helping' ICs control 'IPR technology for ICs'. They have misplaced their efforts. They have controlled the wrong part of the struggle. Control and victory in this case would mean the death of indigenous communities. Which should prevail: control of the IPR regime or survival of the indigenous community doing the controlling? And who should decide?

I am not advocating a patronizing approach to keep the 'purity' of ICs. If we want to assist indigenous communities, let us assist their capacity for self-determination. If they want to enter the IPR regime, that should be their decision. If they want our assistance to protect their biological resources and culture from exploitation, then let us offer an alternative intellectual property protection system more sensitive and appropriate to the worldview and values of indigenous cultures.

That such an undertaking is possible will shortly be exemplified by the proposed Community Intellectual Protection framework being developed by the Third World Network in collaboration with individuals connected with the International Biodiversity and Biotechnology Network. However, developing this new framework necessitated not only a 'technology for whom?' paradigm. It also required an exposé of the ideological dimension of IPR technology and neutralizing and replacing this ideological bias with a new paradigm more harmonious with the culture of ICs.

Thus the new approach to the IPR debate does not negate environmental and socio-political considerations. Instead, in addition to these, the new approach unveils the normally invisible ideological/moral dimension of technology to complete the critique of IPR and bring it to a new plane of deliberation. Otherwise true empowerment cannot be achieved and the empowerment rhetoric animating the 'technology for whom?' paradigm would be dismantled operationally by the cleverly hidden disempowering logic and engine contained at the heart of the IPR approach.

Abstract Spirituality Devoid of Socio-Political Wisdom

Those activists who have a 'science and technology is not neutral' perspective are often naive about and impotent regarding the process and politics of social change. While seeing the value of the social and environmental paradigms, the critics of science are satisfied with concentrating on debunking the outmoded and politically laden paradigms of 'objective' science and technology. As a result their writings lack the detailed policy and program articulations necessary to bring about significant changes in society. They are often marginalized in activists meetings because they have not found a bridge between their incisive critique of the inner logic of science and technology and the burning social and biotechnological questions of the day. Activists from the 'critique of science' stream need to demonstrate how their new perspective can help find a more sustainable solution to the problems that are baffling 150 years of social criticism and 30 years of environmentalism.

Biotechnology and the Seven Dimensions of Sustainable Development

The book's concern for a holistic approach on biotechnology assessment can be summarized in another form. Addressing the social dimension of biotechnology means addressing the issue of social injustice as well as cultural colonialism. Being responsive to the environmental/resource dimension of biotechnology means examining biotechnology's ecological impacts and economic performance. Highlighting the ideological/moral dimension of biotechnology means addressing its fragmented approach, its reduction of the complexities of life to simple biochemical phenomena, and the resulting anti-human and anti-social technologies that ultimately emerge from such a narrow and materialistic view of science.

Therefore, if biotechnology is to have any meaningful role in sustainable development, it should be:

1. socially just and equitable;
2. respectful of cultural pluralism;
3. ecologically sound;
4. economically viable;
5. based on a science which equally considers the material and non-material basis of life;
6. technologically appropriate;
7. empowering of and developing human capacities and potentials.

Having considered the more complex issues, the author would like to update readers regarding current developments in biotechnology and biotechnology products discussed in the book.

Environmental/Resource Impacts

● Insulin, the first commercial biotechnology product, has caused problems for some British users. The genetically-engineered insulin does not give the same physiological signals that natural insulin does. A significant number of British users have collapsed unconscious. No less than 500 diabetics have filed a class action suit against Eli Lilly, manufacturer of the genetically engineered insulin.

● The debate about potential impacts on climate with large scale application of genetically engineered *pseudomonas syringae* remains unresolved. Developers of the product lost interest when they found out that the genetically engineered microbes colonized weeds even better than the economic crops. They recognized the potential problem of weeds growing uncontrollably even in freezing temperatures thereby creating the possibility of additional problems for farmers.

● The spectre of biological warfare still exists especially with the launching of the $5 billion project of the US to map out the human genome. In addition, a consortium of scientists from Europe, US, and Japan has been formed. This consortium, the Human Genome Organization (HUGO), has plans to preserve and study samples of genetic materials from some 722 'endangered' tribes. As before it is still hard to divide knowledge of human genome from actual biowarfare applications. Biological weapons, specially targeting specific genetic traits, can be created from the knowledge generated by these large-scale biotechnology researches.

● In the animal production industry, animals are being forced to fit stressful production systems through genetic engineering. So, though the details of intensification and concentration in the industry may have changed, the substance remains the same.

● The same can be said in agriculture. Pesticide poisoning in the South continues at an accelerated rate. According to the latest World Health Organization (WHO) estimates, 25 million farmers are poisoned by pesticides every year.

Social Impacts

BgH

The concern over the use of bovine growth hormone (BgH) has proven to be justified. In 1993 the European Economic Community imposed a seven-year moratorium on BgH. A similar 1.5 year moratorium was passed by the US Congress. Policy makers were worried that the large scale use of BgH would wipe out small farms and have profound social impacts in the countryside. BgH use has also resulted in the increased incidence of mastitis, a serious disease in milking cows.

Corporate Control

The question of corporate control over the technology is even more urgent today than it was in 1987. For one thing, the many small scale biotechnology 'boutiques' have been all but wiped out as significant players in the field. They have either been gobbled up by giant transnational companies (which simultaneously own significant financial interests in the chemical, seed, pesticide, and even food processing industries), or they have not been able to survive financially in the marketplace.

As a net result it has been estimated that only 11 giant corporations are controlling the research direction of agricultural biotechnology with potentially disastrous results for farmers and the environment. For example, many of these companies are in the final stages of developing herbicide tolerant crops which promise to bring in a new round of environmental abuse. So much for green revolution without chemicals.

The influence of these giant corporations has extended beyond the hundreds of millions of dollars of research money that they have poured into biotechnology. They have also been very active in forging links with governments. They have been trying to win over the sympathy of the state to protect their interest and open up new markets for themselves.

Intellectual Property Rights (IPR)

These maneuvres express themselves clearly in two areas. The first is IPR, specifically the granting of patents on life. In the United States, where there is a law against the patenting of life, corporations have been able to obtain patents on plants, animals, and certain segments of the human genome! Corporate lawyers have achieved this through legalistic redefinition of the law. For example, biotechnologists have been able to obtain patents on life by arguing that their creations are not 'naturally occurring' because they have been altered. Therefore they are exempted from coverage of the law which concerns itself only with 'naturally occurring' life forms. Andrew Kimbrell, Policy Director and Legal Counsel of the Foundation on Economic Trends (FET) in Washington DC, describes this sinister achievement as a 'slippery slope' where scientists and corporations have slowly been able to obtain patents for microbes and, by legal extension, for plants, animals, and human beings despite the existence of a law prohibiting such patents.

Biotechnology corporate lawyers are not content with their achievement in the United States. They now want this type of patent law interpretation to prevail around the world. Thus a second major activity of corporate legal mobilization is Chapter 16 of Agenda 21, the Convention on Biological Diversity, and the Uruguay Round of the General Agreement on Tariffs and Trade (GATT).

During the Earth Summit in Brazil in June 1992, more than 150 countries adopted Agenda 21 and the Convention on Biological Diversity. Chapter 16 of Agenda 21 and the Biodiversity Convention only reinforces the naive and almost religious awe policy makers have of biotechnology. For almost every major environmental problem, policy makers expect a biotechnological solution. A biotechnological fix awaits humanity for problems that are political in nature, problems that arise from the oppression of multitudes by a few. Furthermore these new agreements will force parties to alter their law and executive orders to allow the patenting of life forms.

The recently concluded GATT negotiations also has a provision in Article 27 that allows patenting on life. This section is a direct descendant of the US 'Super 301' provision which calls for 'intellectual property rights' on life. Governments should now expect corporations to demand patents on living organisms which are found within their sovereign territory.

A Second Green Revolution?

In the early days public research institutions followed the cornucopic visions of corporate scientists. They thought of the 10,000 pound cow discussed on page 33. However, in the space of seven years and given the context of the new global agenda espoused by the Earth Summit, public agricultural research institutions have found a born-again concern for the common good. Today, taking up activist language, they say that corporations will not necessarily do research for the poor. They need to be around so that they can defend the interest of the poor. So say some national research institutions and international agricultural research centers (IARCs) including the International Rice Research Institute (IRRI).

But many of these research institutions are surprisingly naive regarding political, economic and, even ecological realities. Their biotechnology activities are bound to be marginally useful at best, harmful at worst, and mostly irrelevant to the real needs and challenges at the farmer level.

IRRI, for example, has publicly stated that it will not undertake research in herbicide tolerant rice. This is laudable. However, it is spending several million dollars to incorporate the endotoxin gene of *Bacillus thuriengensis* (Bt) in rice plants in the hope that this Bt gene will control stemborers, a serious problem in rice. However, many scientists, including some quietly dissenting staff of IRRI, think that the potential benefit for farmers will be short-lived. Thoughtful scientists predict that stemborers will develop resistance to the Bt gene as it has done with pesticides. Worse, the Bt gene may actually develop superstrains of stemborers that can easily devour rice varieties without the Bt resistant gene.

Meanwhile, in terms of relative emphasis and dollar allocations, IRRI is paying marginal attention to natural ecological processes that are capable of maintaining the population of stemborer pests at non-damaging levels. Thousands of farmers all over the Philippines are successfully relying on natural predators and parasites to control stemborers. They are achieving high yields of rice and higher net incomes without using a single drop of pesticides and without waiting for the magical new products of biotechnology. It would definitely be more in keeping with its professed public interest rhetoric if IRRI spent more of its share of globally scarce funding resources on research activities that build upon such successful ecological approaches.

For another example, the Philippine Institute for Biotechnology (BIOTECH) based in Los Banos, Laguna, is asking for more funding to strengthen its capability in phytoproduction. It wants to beat transnational corporations from the North in its own game of export substitution through biotechnology. Northern corporations want, for example, to do away with sugar imports from the South. They can now do this by manufacturing sugar through biotechnological processes which can transform corn starch into sugar. Biotechnology companies can now also create vanilla in industrial vats instead of importing it from Madagascar where close to 100,000 people are employed in growing and marketing natural vanilla.

BIOTECH scientists do not realize that local phytoproduction capability can result in the greater control of local elites over the poor. The rich have more capital, resources and organizational ability to exploit the new biotechnologies. Instead of Northern companies displacing the poor, BIOTECH will provide the tool for Southern elites to destroy the livelihood of the poor.

Phytoproduction and other biotechnologies will not solve the destructive and dehumanizing problems so prevalent in the South and spawned by conventional economic development approaches. Biotechnology will only lull policy makers away from addressing the hard reality that there are limits to the regenerative powers and productivity of the earth and living systems. Biotechnology will also distract the attention of policy makers and hi-tech advocates away from socio-political issues that produce the interrelated structural problems of inequity, poverty, hunger, disempowerment, overpopulation, resource depletion, and environmental destruction.

Ideological Dimension

The increasing number of 'unexpected' 'side effects' and anomalies show the limits of the current paradigm of molecular biology. The gene is only one of many factors governing the emergence of traits in living organisms.

The example of the endotoxin Bt illustrates this very clearly. The Bt endotoxin is capable of killing crop pests. The Bt endotoxin gene has been transferred to corn and other crops. The intent is to reduce the farmers' reliance on pesticides. However, confidential documents obtained reveal that *Clavabacter xylii*, the vector used to transfer the Bt endotoxin gene, causes stunting in corn and dozens of other important agricultural crops.

This current example reinforces a similar point underscored in several places in the book.

Legal Activism and Grassroots Opposition

In addition to the FET, hundreds of other groups around the world have now sprung up to challenge biotechnology as the only option to a future world. FET can now be viewed as a case study of what a determined group can do to challenge the powerful and wealthy lobby advocating for biotechnology. FET with its expanded scope of activities remains important in the struggle to control biotechnology.

Grassroots opposition to biotechnology has also mushroomed throughout the world. But like the more policy oriented groups, these movements are mostly in the North.

However, activists in the South are becoming more active in this issue. They have two reasons to do so. Just like with pesticides, they do not want to be a testing and dumping area for dubious biotechnological experiments and products. And secondly a significant number of southern governments are tantalized by the potential benefits of biotechnology. Just as in the North, southern activists want to shape the agenda of biotechnology before it is dumped on them.

Sustainable Agriculture

The subject of sustainable agriculture has received explosive interest in recent years. Promoters of the green revolution are abandoning the chemical approach to agriculture and are increasingly calling for a shift to sustainable agriculture. Chapter 14 of Agenda 21, signed by over 140 countries, promotes sustainable agriculture. Even the Food and Agriculture Organization (FAO) is questioning the wisdom of the green revolution approach to agriculture. The United Nations Development program (UNDP) is setting up a Sustainable Agriculture Network and Extension Program. The United States Agency for International Development (USAID) has removed pesticides from its aid package. IRRI has banned the use of all Category 1 pesticides in its research farm. Indonesia has banned 57 pesticide formulations, saving itself US$120 million annually.

Large-scale field implementation of bio-dynamic farming and sustainable agriculture are succeeding in the Philippines. Bio-dynamic farming is being successfully used in over 500,000 hectares around the world.

Viewed in the context of these sampling of current developments, this section of the book may appear the most undeveloped. However, I wish to stress that the examples and topics chosen were meant to be indicative and not exhaustive. They were meant to illustrate the points being made in the book. As items illustrating certain principles, the contents of the book remain current.

A more detailed treatment of sustainable agriculture is found in two volumes also to be published by Third World Network in the near future. These are tentatively entitled *Biotechnology or Sustainable Agriculture* and *The Seven Dimensions of Sustainable Agriculture*.

Second Scientific Revolution

Hundreds of articles and dozens of new books are being published every year regarding the 'second scientific revolution'. One group in the Philippines, the Center for Alternative Development Initiatives (CADI), is currently drawing up the implications for sustainable development of these radical developments in science. A book will be published in 1994 to document this effort. A similar organization, the Elmwood Institute, has been set up in the United States. In England, a similar organization has been recently established. An international conference on the New Biology and its implications for biotechnology is scheduled to be held in Penang, Malaysia, in July 1994.

Again, just like sustainable agriculture, the many new developments in this area have reinforced the arguments and conclusions discussed in the book.

The biotechnology revolution is upon us. It promises to be the new economic infrastructure of the post-industrial era. We have to enter into the labyrinths of its hidden agenda, grab the beast by the horns, and transform it to truly serve the interests of nature, society and the human spirit.

Part I
Biotechnology: A Double-Edged Sword

CHAPTER 1

Genetic Engineering: A New Magic Bullet?

During the past centuries, technological mastery over the inorganic realm has given rise to the Industrial Age and to the present contours of contemporary civilization. The mining, extraction, purification, and transformation of the planet's inorganic dowry of minerals and fossil fuels into human utilities have given birth to the vast and intricate web of global economic interdependencies that lace the planet. Now that humanity has appropriated and consumed the inorganic being of Nature, it is set to embark on a new and even more tantalizing quest: the engineering and redesigning of the earth's living heritage into a second genesis. Humanity is stepping into the portals of a new Eden, the Biotechnological Civilization.

Proponents broadly define biotechnology as 'any technique that uses living organisms (or part of organisms) to make or modify products, to improve plants or animals, or to develop micro-organisms for specific uses'. By giving this definition, proponents would like to assure the general public that there is nothing essentially new or different about the novel forms of biotechnologies that have emerged during the last decade. For these proponents, the new biotechnologies, including cell fusion, and genetic engineering, are simply a continuation of a long historical process of continued manipulation of the living world to satisfy human needs. As the Office of Technology Assessment of the Congress of the United States puts it: 'Biotechnology is the most recent phase in a historical continuum of the use of biological organisms for practical purposes.'

It is clear, however, that, with the newer forms of biotechnology, humanity has crossed the threshold of a brave new world. In the early 1970s, Stanley Cohen of Stanford University and Herbert Boyer of the University of California ripped the veil that separates species and created a new life form that had never existed in Nature. The technique is called recombinant DNA (rDNA) and its invention rivals the importance of the discovery of fire itself. The 'eighth day of creation' has begun. Man now 'play God', disarranging and recombining gene fragments of unrelated species at will to design, for better or for worse, new organisms for utilitarian ends.

The events that occurred at Wall Street on 14 October 1980 epitomize the new-found fascination for the technological invasion of the sacred preserves of life. On that day, Genentech became the first privately held genetic engineering company to offer its stocks to the general public. Genentech offered over one million shares of stocks at $35 per share. Within the first 20 minutes of trading, the Genentech stocks commanded $89 per share, a gain of over 100% – a Wall Street record. By the time the clamour at the trading floors of Wall Street ended, the young biotechnology firm garnered $36 million and was valued at $532 million. The remarkable thing about the whole affair was that Genentech had yet to offer a single product into the marketplace.

Cornucopic visions of the fruits of biotechnology flourish with amazing abandon. Some firms predict the development of a 10,000 pound cow the size of a small elephant as a result of transferring, via cell fusion, whale growth hormone genes into the genome of cows. Others, seeing a tremendous use for genetic engineering and biotechnology in farming, prophesy a new and greener revolution in agricultural productivity and the ultimate conquest of world hunger.

Cornucopic fantasies aside, genetic engineering will probably find its first important applications in the pharmaceutical industry. Human insulin, for example, is now being mass produced by combining the human gene which governs insulin production with the genetic system of a bacteria. The resulting drug is being used to treat diabetics.

By the year 2000, analysts predict a $50 billion market for new biotechnology products. With visions of raking in millions of dollars and doing good for humanity, scientists, businessmen and entrepreneurs have established hundreds of biotechnology firms around the world.

Unfortunately, with any technological development, costs accompany benefits. Even in apparently benign applications, the impact of the new recombinant DNA technologies can be potentially devastating.

For example, *Pseudomonas syringae*, a bacteria which lives on the leaf surface of plants, secretes a protein substance which acts as a nucleus for the formation of ice crystals. Genetic engineers have deleted the gene connected with this ice-nucleating capability in the hope of preventing frost damage to agricultural crops. However, scientific investigations have shown that *P. syringae* performs a vital role in the triggering of rainfall. Replacement of natural *P. syringae* by the genetically-engineered 'ice-minus' *P. syringae* on a large scale can create extensive damage by altering weather patterns.

This new technology can also be misused in other ways. Both the US Department of Defense and their Soviet counterparts are currently engaged in a new arms race which uses genetic engineering to develop defensive biological warfare capabilities. For example, the gene which expresses the toxin of cobra venom is being transferred into *E. Coli*, a bacteria which lives in human intestines. Similar splicing experiments are going on with other deadly pathogens including plague and encephalitis. The use of recombinant DNA technology for the creation of novel biological toxins could rival the perils of nuclear weaponry in a few years.

CHAPTER 2

Three Dimensions Of Technology

Contemporary civilization is in a desperate struggle with the imperatives of technology. There are cries for a reintegration of religion with science to help stem the tide of technological imperialism. There are pleas for a more 'emphathetic knowledge': a knowledge for participation rather than instrumental control. There are serious calls for a 'predictive ecology' that will provide future knowledge of the impact of technologies on the environment in advance of their execution. There are even articulations of a 'deep ecology' perspective which hopes to radically arrest man's domination over Nature. In addition, court litigations and grassroots organizing have been undertaken to regulate and even stop some of the more menacing features of humanity's drive towards the creation of a bioengineered Garden of Eden.

Is technology really neutral, easily malleable to human desires and purposes? Or does technology have an inner logic, which gradually numbs and enslaves the human body, soul, and spirit while it offers bountiful fruits and gifts? Does Nature, including human beings, have an 'inside' and, if so, what are the effects of technology on the inner sanctum of Nature and Humanity?

In a statement that exemplifies the prevailing opinion on the central issue of assessing the impact of and controlling technology, David Sarnoff says:

> We are too prone to make technological instruments the
> scapegoats for the sins of those who wield them. The
> products of modern science are not in themselves good or
> bad; it is the way they are used that determines their value.

The purveyors of technique believe that technology serves the
purposes defined by those who create them. Critics, on the
other hand, contend that technology has its own logic which
defy those of their creators. Still others contend that redistribu-
tion of power and social control will be enough to tame technology.

All these different viewpoints have their inherent worth and
truth. They articulate different perspectives needed to assess
the impact of and control technology.

First, technology, manifesting itself through human agency, is
saturated with a worldview and its attendant value system.
Through technology, the material world is reconstituted and
organized according to a dominant or controlling value or
objective. This is the true realm of the inner logic of technology
which some critics have alluded to. We can call this the **ideo-
logical/moral dimension** of technology.

Take the case of tobacco plants which have been genetically
engineered to resist herbicide damage. David Sarnoff and
people who think like him will consider this technology to be
beneficial because it increases tobacco yields.

But oblivious to the David Sarnoffs are the larger questions
related to the inner logic of **substitutive technology** in agriculture. The implicit logic of genetically engineered herbicide
tolerant crops declares that it is good to continue substituting

the toxic products of biochemistry in place of alternative practices that control weeds naturally; that better and bigger crops
are to be pursued even if there is adverse impact on soil, water,
wildlife and human beings; that technologies based on a science
premised on a methodological draining of living qualities out of
Nature and designed to dominate and control natural processes
are the only sure pathways to agricultural progress.

However, as agricultural historians Wolfgang Krohn and Wolf
Schaefer correctly point out:

> [I]n agricultural chemistry, the social purpose is not the
> **result** of scientific knowledge but the **condition** of scien-
> tific inquiry. Agricultura¹ chemistry does not provide
> insights into **why** agriculture functions but rather consti-
> tutes a design of **how it must** function. [Emphasis in the
> original.] ... [T]he science of agriculture is a theory about
> the most rational organizing of nature to satisfy human
> needs and at the same time a science about the rationality
> of human needs **vis-á-vis** nature. (Emphasis added.)

This aspect can also be called the 'Trojan Horse' dimension of all
technologies including biotechnology. Alien and foreign modes
of thoughts and values are hidden inside and carried over into
other cultures with every piece of equipment and technique
that is imported. Destructive impact of one culture on another
is the result of an uncritical acceptance of technology especially
in cases where only the visible benefits of the technology are
emphasized and promoted. Accusations including 'cultural
imperialism' are semi-conscious articulations of experiencing
one's values eroding before the ideology embedded in imported technologies.

Second, the ideological and moral content behind a technology
needs a specific milieu of biophysical forces and substances for

its embodiment. We can call this the **resource/environmental dimension** of technology. It is the context of the actual visible form that the technology assumes in the world. Implicit in this realm are the specific laws which govern the operation of the technology in the biophysical world. If we fail to comprehend and participate in the vast web of living interrelationships with Nature, the introduction of a technology perceived to be benign can result in widespread adverse impact on human health and the environment.

For example, genetic engineers are currently transferring HgH genes into livestock to create bigger and faster-growing farm animals such as the so-called 'super cows'. However, these gene engineers implicitly or explicitly follow a set of breeding goals and criteria which build upon current intensive animal production practices. When their genetically altered breed of livestock reaches commercialization stage, these genetic engineers will aggravate the current technology-induced adverse impact on the human environment. As will be seen in greater detail, this impact includes pollution of drinking water, scientist and farmer-induced livestock diseases and cruelty, and contamination of the human diet with toxic and cancer-causing chemicals, and narrowing the genetic diversity of farm animals.

Technology has a third dimension. The idea behind a technology needs a social context to manifest itself. There must be individuals and institutions which will refine the idea and apply it in a particular field. The idea and value embedded in a technology must enter the dynamics of the economic-political-cultural structure of the specific country trying to embody a technology. This social structure includes the prevailing worldview sanctified in the culture, the political logic and arrangements designed to address or ignore equity issues, and the prevailing practices of economic institutions as they seek to appropriate the earth for whatever human ends they see fit.

This complex collective is the **social dimension** of technology. Independent Marxist scholars are particularly perceptive in identifying the impact of technology on the social fabric of a society.

For example, a new genetically engineered product called BgH can increase milk production by up to 40%. A Cornell University study, however, has concluded that up to 30% of all the dairy farms in the United States will be forced out of business within 36 months after BgH is first introduced into the marketplace. Entire dairy farming communities will be financially decimated with the introduction of BgH into the market.

The question arises: Who determines how the rural landscape of America will look like in the year 2000? What social arrangements shall be undertaken to equitably resolve this problem?

Or take the case of a live pseudorabies virus vaccine created with the power of recombinant DNA. Manufacturers and scientists have praised this new vaccine as being more precise and effective than conventional ones. The US Department of Agriculture (USDA) approved the use of this vaccine without the proper regulatory oversight. Because of litigation pressure from the FET, the USDA was forced to suspend the commercial license of TechAmerica to manufacture and market this vaccine.

What would have happened if the vaccine were not safe? Can the federal agencies be trusted to properly regulate biotechnology? Can the biotechnology industry be trusted to police itself when, at the dawn of this technology, one of its kind (Advanced Genetic Sciences) was fined a maximum amount of $20,000 for falsification of data and secretly releasing gene altered bacteria into the environment?

Clearly, then, controlling all technologies, including biotechnology, and using it for good requires an intimate understanding of these three dimensions of technology. Focusing on pure technology alone, what it can do, obviously neglects the political, ideological, and moral logics of the technology. Benign technology will always remain an illusion unless all three dimensions are addressed. The impact of technology must be weighed on all three levels.

Keeping these three dimensions of technology in mind, I would now like to examine the potential impact of genetic engineering and biotechnology in agriculture. I am limiting myself to agriculture because many of the upcoming applications of biotechnology will be in farming. Furthermore, agriculture is the key social and economic sector of most developing countries.

Part II
The Biotechnology Revolution in Agriculture: Environment and Resources Impacts

CHAPTER 3

Effects of Present Intensive
Animal Production

As we have seen, all technologies, including biotechnology, do not exist in a vacuum. Agricultural biotechnologies presuppose and build upon much of the current ideas, values, social structure, techniques, and practices of capital and chemical intensive agriculture. The implicit goals and values embedded in modern agriculture subtly govern every step in the development of the new agricultural biotechnologies. Unless there is a drastic revision of much of the current thinking and practices which animate the research and development of new biotechnologies for agriculture, one can confidently expect to find an aggravation and acceleration of the current environmental and social problems associated with modern agriculture.

A detailed case study of the proposed introduction of biotechnology in intensive animal production systems will exemplify the mutually reinforcing dynamics which exist between conventional agricultural practices and the new biotechnologies. The case study will also indicate the serious environmental and social consequences that await humanity with the introduction of biotechnologies in a non-sustainable agricultural system which continues on its present course of destruction. Furthermore this case study will guide us in exploring the tremendous impact that await us when biotechnology is introduced into other areas of agriculture.

Existing Resource and Environmental Impacts of Intensive Animal Production

The US animal production system will serve as a good example. It contains many lessons for developing countries which seek to emulate what has been achieved in the United States. In addition, because it is fairly advanced in a certain direction, the consequences are also more visible and obvious.

In the past 50 years, the poultry industry has been transformed from a backyard operation of tens of thousands of small businesses producing a few dozen birds to a few large, hyper-capitalized, almost fully automated systems housing tens of thousands of birds in small confined areas. Many individuals enamoured with the promise of high technology in farming consider this to be an example of the bright successes of modern farming methods.

Ken Holleman, USDA Program Leader, Poultry Science, Extension Service, who characterizes this miracle of transformation as a modern 'Cinderella Story', describes the historical evolution of the modern poultry industry.

> Farmyard scenes have changed considerably over the past half century, but the most dramatic change is with poultry. No more flocks of 100 or 200 hens scratching in the barnyard and going in to roost before sundown. No more dressing a couple of spring fryers early Sunday morning. No more eggs brought to the grocery store for credit to the family account.
>
> Poultry historically was part of the family farm. Chicken and eggs (even turkeys at times) were part of our heritage of being self-sufficient, just as were the milk cow, the pigs being fattened, fruit trees, and the vegetable garden. In

general, each family produced what poultry products it could, ate what it needed, and sold what was left over.

The entire poultry industry is a far cry from what it used to be. Eggs are produced under controlled conditions by hens capable of laying over 250 eggs each per year....

Broilers are produced on highly specialized farms that do little else. **Specially bred birds** are fed rations formulated to produce optimum growth, uniformity, quality, and even the most desirable skin colour in less than eight weeks on two pounds of feed for each pound of chicken. The birds are processed completely even to being cut up, deboned, and packaged prior to distribution for consumer purchase.

Turkeys are an equally phenomenal story. Modern turkeys are white feathered, **of such broad meaty conformation that they can't even mate naturally,** and reach market weights in 14 to 22 weeks of age on three pounds of feed per pound of turkey. They are grown in flocks of 5,000 to 50,000 many in total confinement.

These successes in American agriculture have been achieved through a partnership effort. Research has led the way by providing the basis for making changes. **Ideas that researchers developed have been taken by industry and turned into efficient production and processing technology....**

Extension has joined researchers in taking research and applying it to commercial conditions. This partnership of research, extension, and industry has made the poultry industry a shining example of government programs and the free enterprise system. (Emphasis added.)

Translating this pean to modern animal production in terms of facts and figures reveals the reality behind the image. Concentration and intensification is very dramatic with chicken egg and poultry meat production.

In 1974, there were a total of 303,023 egg farms housing a total of 285 million laying chickens in the United States. Of the 303,023 egg farms, 5,167 farms (or 1.7%) with 20,000 birds or more per farm, accounted for two-thirds of the total number of birds. Ninety-three percent (93%) of the total output comes from 5.5% of farms. Ninety-three percent of birds or some 265 million laying chickens were raised in some form of mechanization and automation and controlled housing conditions. Typical production units increasingly 'have been converted from floor to cage operations and cage operations now predominate'. It is projected by USDA economists that average flock sizes by the mid-to-late 1990s may be more than 75% larger than the 1974 figures.

The intensity and concentration in the broiler production industry is even greater than the chicken egg industry. In 1974, 32,744 farms produced 2.551 billion commercial broilers. The average size of the farms was 76,915 broilers per farm. There were more than 50% of these farms, or 16,534 farms, which sold 60,000 or more broilers per farm. Collectively, these 50% or so of broiler farms accounted for 89.7% of total output. 'More batches of broilers are being raised per year in a given house capacity, and space per bird has been reduced.' Confinement systems dominate the rearing of birds. Some 2.2 billion birds were raised in some form of intensive and confined systems. As for the future, USDA economists recognize that there 'is little economic basis for assuming a dissolution of the operating linkages between input-supplying, production, and marketing' which have produced the intensive broiler production system which dominates the chicken meat industry today. Average flock sizes for commercial broiler production were projected to reach over 100,000 birds per farm by the year 1985.

Similar revolutionary changes have occurred in the United States in other areas of animal farming, including beef, dairy, turkey, and pork production.

In 1974, total beef production was around 23.6 billion pounds, of which 6.2 billion pounds, or 27% were 'fed beef', a specialized operation where feeder cattle are fed grain in confinement to condition and fatten them for the 'fed beef' market. By 1977, large commercial feedlots have developed so rapidly that only 422 feedlots, each of which averaged 30,000 heads marketed a year, accounted for 12.9 million heads, or more than 50% of all fed cattle for that year. Several feedlot farms have a one-time capacity in excess of 100,000 feeder cattle. Although beef cattle numbers increased by 8 million heads between 1964 and 1974, a total of 300,000 farms and ranches stopped operation. The future holds a trend towards larger feedlot sizes, probably clustering around a feedlot size of 40,000 to 50,000 heads.

In the dairy industry, a total of 10.6 million cows were raised in approximately 403,000 farms in 1974. Thirteen percent of these milk cows were raised in farms that had herd sizes of 100 cows or more. Some large scale drylot operations had 2,000 cows per herd and as many as 10,000 cows per herd have been established in California, Arizona, and Florida. Twenty-six percent of milk cows, or 2.8 million cows, were raised in 3.6% of farms. The trend towards larger and fewer dairy farms with large incomes is expected to continue.

The intensity of production of turkey meat is similar, although not as dramatic as with broiler production. In 1974, there were 4,407 turkey farms which produced 125 million turkeys. The average number of turkeys per farm was 28,305. Some 40% or 1,763 farms, selling 16,000 or more turkeys, accounted for 91.6% of total output. As in broiler production more batches of turkeys are being raised per year and on less space per bird. Range rearing of turkeys is rapidly giving way to semiconfinement and total confinement systems, requiring tens of millions of turkeys to be raised in intensive production systems. As with broilers, the forces, including mechanization and technological innovation, which have produced intensive turkey production systems, will most likely be still operative. USDA economists predicted flock sizes averaging 42,000 turkeys per farm by 1985, a 50% increase in intensification as compared to the structure of the turkey industry in 1974.

In 1979, the total number of farms selling pigs was a little over 300,000. These produced around 12 to 15 billion pounds (carcass weight) of pork a year. It is estimated that farmers selling 1,000 heads of pigs or more annually accounted for about 40% of total production for that year. There are some 3,000 producers whose annual sales of slaughtered hogs range from 2,500 to 15,000 heads. These account for one-sixth of total national production. These leading hog farms 'reflect an extension of on going trends in terms of increasing size of hog enterprises, adoption of technology, and enterprise specialization.'

As for the future, USDA scientists predict that 'most of the factors that promoted changes in US hog production during the last 10 to 20 years appear likely to prevail for the remainder of the century.... The current consensus is that long-term success in hog production will require use of the most advanced production technologies, especially in the area of facilities. Under present conditions, this would imply steady and rapid continuation of the trend to relatively large, fully enclosed, high-density, intensively utilized hog housing furnished with mechanical feed preparation and distribution equipment, mechanically automated ventilating, heating, and air conditioning equipment, and pit storage for months of wastes handled mechanically in liquid form... By the turn of the century, ... units selling 1,000 or more hogs annually may provide three-fourths of the hogs sold.'

It is clear from the above descriptions that US animal production systems have dramatically and rapidly altered through the last few decades. There are fewer and larger farming units accounting for a great majority of total production. **Billions** of birds, hogs, and cattle are raised in intensive, high-density, automated and mechanized feedlot or containment systems. USDA scientists predict not only a continuation of this trend, but also further intensification and concentration of the present structure of animal agriculture. On this structure is built the 'success' story of American animal farming. Unfortunately, on this same structure, emanates the large-scale adverse environmental and human impact of US animal production.

Adverse Impacts of Animal Waste on Environment

In the past, animals were widely dispersed over large areas where their wastes were distributed over the land. Because animals are increasingly being raised in larger and more highly concentrated units, the disposal of animal wastes has become a major problem, subject to different state and federal regulations. The extent of the problems is enormous.

All farm animals in the US produce approximately 2 billion tons of solid and liquid manure per year. This is equivalent to the total amount of faeces and waste generated by 2 billion people per year, or roughly 41% of the world's population. Approximately one half of this amount is produced in confinement operations.

Another way of envisioning the enormous waste management problem is to look at a feedlot operation which averages 30,000 heads of cattle a year. There were approximately 422 such operations in the United States in 1979. A 30,000 head feedlot operation generates as much nitrogen load on soil and water as a city with a population of 250,000 people. Four hundred and twenty-two such operations mean managing the equivalent nitrogen load of 422 cities with 250,000 residents each. This is equivalent to the amount of nitrogen wastes generated by 105.5 million people, roughly close to half the population of the United States at that time.

Solid and liquid wastes, not handled expediently and properly, create pollution and health problems. The nitrogen from animal wastes can seep into aquifers and contaminate the water supply of communities which rely on groundwater for their drinking needs. This nitrogen contamination can cause a health hazard called *methemoglobinemia*. This is a serious disease which results from nitrite nitrogen poisoning. Many rural water sources now exceed the safety limit of 10 parts per million. Animal waste is one source of the pollution. Already a number of human deaths have been recorded from *methemoglobinemia*. Contamination of the water supply with harmful bacteria and chemicals is also a hazard arising from intensive animal production methods.

Runoff from animal wastes can also cause eutrophication of lakes and coastal marine areas, such as the Chesapeake Bay near Washington DC. Eutrophication results from the increased production of organic matter in the water system due to an increased supply of either nitrogen, phosphorus, and other nutrients. When this living biomass dies, its decomposition taxes the oxygen supply of the water. Eutrophication can alter the balance between plant and animal life in these waters. In addition foul smelling lakes can result, contributing to air pollution. In extreme cases, fish, oysters, and other sources of human food can die.

Pollution of air is another impact of animal wastes. Intensive farm operations generate foul odour. In addition flies are attracted to the wastes by the odour. The presence of flies adds another dimension to the health problems associated with animal wastes in 'factory farms'. The problem of foul odour has been so bad in certain instances that neighbours have complained and sued operators of feedlots or pig factories. A Kansas pig factory was forced to shut down by state authorities because of active intervention by neighbours. A pig producer summed up best the dilemma faced by operators of intensive animal farming systems.

> We've got two routes to go. Either disperse the livestock so we don't have to disperse the waste or concentrate the livestock and have problems dispersing the waste.

These comments bring us to a serious environmental impact scarcely recognized as being related to intensified animal production systems. This is the problem of soil erosion. In the past, animals were an integral part of the total farming operation. Therefore their wastes were utilized on the farm to improve the physical and biological characteristics which enhance soil fertility and protect the soils from eroding. With the specialization of agriculture, animals were divorced from the diversified farms and concentrated in small areas. In some feedlot operations, for example, 30,000 animals are concentrated in areas as small as 25 acres. In the past these 30,000 animals would require 30,000 or more acres depending on soil and environmental conditions. The separation of animals from the farm, along with other factors including the neglect of crop rotation schemes and more concentration on row crops like corn, has led to an increase in soil erosion.

The 1980 USDA *Report and Recommendations on Organic Farming*, for example, has pointed out that animals 'comprise an essential part of most organic farms, especially on the large full-time family farms in the grain producing areas.... Organic agriculture also strongly emphasizes the application of manure and other organic materials to maintain or increase the soil organic matter content which, in turn, increases water infiltration and storage, decreases nutrient and pesticide runoff, and reduces soil erosion.'

With the separation of animals from the totality of the farming operation, what was once a resource, helping reduce erosion and providing nutrients for crops, is now a scourge, polluting the environment and endangering the existence of wildlife and human communities.

Adverse Impacts of Intensive Animal Production on Human Health

There is widespread recognition that present-day intensive animal husbandry practices which increasingly characterize livestock production and dominate poultry operations would be impossible without the use of antibiotics like penicillin.

Dr H.S. Siegel, poultry expert at USDA, observes that 'increases in acute infectious diseases ... [which] have accompanied the rise of monocultural animal agriculture have been largely controlled by vaccination, therapeutic agents, and modern sanitary practices.'

In hogs, for example, USDA scientists R.N. Van Arsdall and H.C. Gilliam explain that routine use of antibiotics and related antibacterial drugs 'help suppress and prevent the spread of diseases among hogs'. In addition, Van Arsdall and Gilliam project that curtailing the use of antibiotics and related drugs will have a significant impact on the intensive structure of hog industry. According to Van Arsdall and Gilliam:

Many producers believe that the risks of catastrophic losses to disease among hogs maintained in large, high-density facilities would be unacceptably great without the protection afforded by antibiotic feed additives. The loss of several drugs that have been perceived as important contributors to the development of concentrated hog production could, at least temporarily slow the trend to total confinement, centralized facilities.

The industry concurs with these observations. A pig producer has said, for example, that: 'One reason large confinement systems have worked is because of antibiotics. Without antibiotics it would be hard to have these larger systems and crowd pigs as we do in some cases.'

Unfortunately, one of the most basic ecological laws is that there is no free lunch in nature. Scientists have discovered that a strong possibility exists for adverse impact on human health due to the development of resistant strains of bacteria to human therapeutic use of antibiotics resulting from the consumption of livestock products tainted with antibiotics.

In August 1984, Dr Scott Holmberg and others at the Centers for Disease Control (CDC) published in *Science* strong evidence that supported the concerns of scientists about the adverse impact on human health of antibiotics used in modern animal production systems.

The importance and origin of antimicrobial-resistance Salmonella infections were examined in 52 outbreaks investigated by the Centers for Disease Control between 1971 and 1983. The case fatality rate was higher for patients infected with antimicrobial-resistant Salmonella (4.2%) than for those with antimicrobial sensitive infections (0.2%). In the 38 outbreaks with identified sources, food animals were the source of 11 (69%) of 16 resistant and 6 (46%) of 13 sensitive outbreak strains.

Based on their investigations, Dr Holmberg and colleagues concluded that:

Antimicrobial-resistant enteric bacteria frequently arise from food animals and can cause serious infections in humans.

There are additional hazards to human health as a result of intensive animal production systems. A detailed investigation by the General Accounting Office (GAO) of the US Congress revealed hazardous residue in meat which seriously endangers human health: animal drugs (antibiotics), pesticides, environmental contaminants, and other carcinogenic substances. Many of the substances used in sustaining intensive animal production systems are known to cause or are suspected of causing cancer, birth defects, reduced fertility, reproduction effects, neurotoxicity, or other toxic effects.

The amount of contamination is staggering. In 1976, the total weight of animals slaughtered was 26,215,945 tons. The GAO estimated that 14% or **3.6 million tons** of raw meat was contaminated with toxic substances. Some of the contaminants included pesticides and other substances that have been banned, or are in the process of being cancelled for use, including DDT, aldrin, heptachlor, dieldrin, 2,4,5-T and silvex. To make matters worse, most of these dangerous contaminants are not even included in USDA's monitoring program.

The US Food and Drug Administration (FDA) has already banned the use of diethylstilbestrol (DES), a synthetic growth hormone used in animal production. Scientific tests have established that DES is a human carcinogen.

Adverse Impacts of Intensive Production Methods on Animals

The impacts of animal production practices on farm animals have to be considered in and of themselves. There is essentially no difference between the random impacts of intensive animal production practices on animals in the environment and the non-random and inevitable impact of these practices on farm animals themselves.

Through a combination of genetics and environmental manipulation, intensive production of animals became possible. Unfortunately, as is well known by any breeder, selection of one set of traits is attained only at the expense, neglect, and underdevelopment of other clusters of traits which may be equally important in the total performance of the breed.

Harvard Professor Ernst Mayr, one of the founders of modern evolutionary theory in biology, points to this danger in an emphatic way.

> Obviously any drastic improvement under selection must seriously deplete the store of genetic variability .... The most frequent correlated response to one-sided selection is a drop in general fitness.

A good example of this phenomenon is the success of the USDA program in breeding the whitebreasted turkey. Ken Holleman, Poultry Science Program Leader of USDA's Extension Service, enthusiastically reports:

> Turkeys are an equally phenomenal story. Modern turkeys are white feathered, of such broad meaty conformation that they can't even mate naturally.

Instead of pursuing a more balanced breeding program, however, a technological solution is engineered, reproduction via artificial insemination.

There is increasing evidence that the imbalanced breeding program of USDA is contributing to the emergence of 'production diseases' in animal farms. Focusing on one-sided productivity gains induces the appearance of 'production diseases', a major environmental impact of intensive animal production systems.

As early as 1974, Sainsbury has pointed to the connection between the push for productivity and the greater incidence of metabolic disorders in farm animals. Reiland has done studies that show accelerated growth can lead to osteochondrosis in pigs. USDA's H. Siegel has observed a direct correlation between rapid growth and lameness in animals. There are also reports that decline of fertility in farm animals is directly related to their rapid growth.

This observation strongly suggests that USDA breeding programs geared towards pure productivity criteria (faster growth rates, better fed conversion ratios, etc.) may be undermining the fertility and reproductive efficiency of farm animals, a problem which costs the animal production industry tens of millions of dollars – a major economic and animal health impact. In addition, animals are subjected to new forms of cruelty and health hazards from the emergence of 'production diseases' that have increasingly characterized modern intensive animal production methods.

USDA acknowledges the problem of 'production diseases'.

Other losses are from 'production diseases', which often produce no recognizable clinical signs of disease but do lower productive efficiency. As a class, they are complex epidemiologically and have infectious, toxic, genetic, metabolic, and nutritional etiologies, or combinations thereof. They generally result from several etiological factors that act in concert with environmental and production factors. This class of diseases includes infectious complexes, reproductive disorders, stress-related syndromes, parasites and insect infestations, and combinations of two or more thereof.

A few examples of these production diseases are:

dairy cows: mastitis, metritis, infertility, claw injuries, and 'foot rot'

calves: respiratory diseases, scours, leg damage, and leg weakness

sows: MMA syndrome (lactation failure), leg injuries, and anoestrus

pigs: enhanced mortality, respiratory diseases, scours, claw injuries, aggressiveness, and leg weakness.

USDA scientist H. Siegel recognizes the biological costs that appear as 'reduced growth or productivity' as a result of modern intensive animal husbandry practices.

There also seems to be an increase in the so-called 'noninfectious' diseases (i.e. those not caused by specific disease organisms). These may appear to be physical, such as twisted leg syndrome in broiler chickens or digestive dysfunction in cattle, or they may appear behavioural, such as feather-picking chickens and tail-biting in pigs. Altogether, there seems to be a shift from diseases caused by a single agent (monocausal) to those in which one or more disease agents, the environment, and the individual's susceptibility interact (multicausal).

The increases in chronic infectious and non-infectious disease have been attributed to modern production practices, because not only do these practices seem to impose greater infection pressure on the animal population, but they also produce changes in the climatic and behavioural environment to which the animal species has not genetically adapted.

Adverse Impacts of Intensive Production on Animal Germplasm Diversity

In 1984, the Council for Agricultural Science and Technology (CAST), with some participation from USDA scientists, issued a report pointing to the increasing danger to animal production of a trend towards a loss of genetic diversity. The report, *Animal Germplasm Preservation and Utilization in Agriculture*, (hereinafter 'CAST Report') warned:

The intensification of animal production that has occurred as part of the evolving food production system generally reduces the genetic diversity of animal germplasm resources. Intensive systems are most productive when the animals have the genetic potential for favourable response to the environments provided. The increasingly intensive systems that have characterized the poultry industry for more than 30 years and, more recently, the swine industry, have favoured greater uniformity of breeding stocks for commercial production. In dairy cattle, the economic factors of production and marketing that favour maximum output of fluid milk per cow have led to a dairy industry in which more than 90% of current production is accounted for by the Holstein breed ....

On a global basis, it seems likely that the normal evolution of animal agriculture through application of new production technologies will cause a gradual reduction of genetic variability in the important animal food and fibre species. This trend toward loss of genetic variation is expected to continue unless programs are developed that foster maintenance of potentially useful stocks that may not have current commercial value ....

Reasonable free access to animal germplasm from other parts of the world is important for the future of US animal production. In several species, the genetic diversity available in the United States may not be adequate to improve performance in response to changing production resources and market requirements.

The loss of genetic diversity is a very serious problem. Genetic uniformity makes animal production systems vulnerable to changing biophysical and social environments.

On 9 November 1983, the USDA declared a state of 'extraordinary emergency' due to an outbreak of avian flu among poultry flocks in Pennsylvania. By January 1984, USDA declared a state of extraordinary emergency applicable to any area as the disease continued to spread to New Jersey, Virginia and Maryland. The genetic, chemical and drug defense system of the poultry industry were breached by the avian flu. By the time the disease was controlled, 12 million poultry animals had to be destroyed. In Pennsylvania alone, farmers lost $51.9 million. The USDA's Commodity Credit Corporation transferred $61.7 million to USDA's Animal and Plant Health Inspection Service to help eradicate the disease. Of this amount, the USDA paid a total of $41.1 million in indemnities to poultry farmers whose flocks were destroyed to stop the spread of the disease.

The avian flu virus spread rapidly because of the relative genetic uniformity of poultry breeds. The dynamics involved is similar to the outbreak of a virulent strain of fungus which wiped out 710 million bushels or 15% of the US corn crop in 1970. The fungus had broken through the defenses of the corn crop which had a highly uniform cytoplasm.

The problem of genetic uniformity in animals is further exemplified by the case of the US dairy cattle herd. The CAST Report explains the basis for the concern:

> The lack of genetic diversity and the loss of germplasm resources could become serious in dairy cattle, both nationally and internationally. In the United States, there is a continuing trend towards the use of only one breed, the Holstein, primarily because of superiority in whole-milk production per cow. The proportion of Holsteins in all US dairy cattle registration was 79% in 1981....

> Although the Holstein breed is clearly superior in whole-milk production per cow, this advantage is dependent upon a high level of concentrate feeding and a pricing policy that inadvertently favours low milk - solids content. Thus, a marked increase in the price of concentrate and by-product feeds relative to forages or whole-milk could reduce the economic advantage of the Holstein breed. Similarly, a change in milk-pricing policy favouring higher total solids content would reduce the superiority of the Holstein breed and increase the advantage from cross-breeding.... Genetic resistance to mastitis or other diseases could increase in importance as a result of withdrawal of specific antibiotics or other therapeutic agents from the market, or the development of resistant strains of pathogens. Any one or a combination of these factors could create a need for dairy cattle germplasm not available within a single dominant breed.

Because of the demonstrated superiority of the Holstein breed, 'extensive importation' by European and semitropical countries is displacing the existing dairy breeds in those countries. If this trend continues, global germplasm diversity of dairy cattle will create a major problem for the continued survival of the industry.

As a guide to the future, the CAST Report gives the following guidelines that have very important ramifications for USDA breeding and 'animal productivity' programs:

> Maintenance of a high level of genetic variation in animal germplasm resources is necessary to achieve continued balance among the biological characteristics of commercial breeding stocks, the production environment most favoured by technological and economic factors, and the market requirements for animal products .... Research has demonstrated that animal population that rank in a particular order in performance for economic characters in a given setting may rank differently under different nutritional and managerial conditions ....

> In general, modification of all components of the physical environment to the degree required to achieve **maximum** production from animals of a given strain is not economically feasible. A practical objective is to **optimize** the conversion of production resources into animal products by synchronizing the biological characteristics of the animal germplasm resources with the production environment most favoured by technological and economic factors. Anticipated adjustments in the availability and cost of production resources and anticipated changes in market requirements for animal products will increase the demand for germplasm resources to shift the biological characteristics of commercial breeding stocks.

CHAPTER 4

Why Biotechnology Worsens Adverse Effects of Intensive Animal Production

Through the use of recombinant DNA technologies, scientists hope to continue the historical process of breeding even more productive livestock and poultry, including earlier maturing, faster growing, larger and/or higher yielding animals. They expect these animals to yield greater quantities and in certain respects, higher quality meat, milk, eggs, and other animal products for food and other purposes, often over shorter periods of time, than did their predecessor breeds.

However, the goals of biotechnologists seldom, if ever, call into question the set of assumptions and structures that have created the present system of intensive animal production. It is true that bigger and faster growing livestock will be produced under these intensive systems. However, it is equally true that bigger and greater adverse impacts on the human environment will of necessity accompany the introduction of biotechnology into animal production.

Breeding programs which utilize biotechnology are crucial in the chain of events which ultimately lead to the adverse impacts on the human environment described above. In any breeding program, a set of implicit or explicit criteria guides and governs the selection progress. These criteria will determine the form, function, and capabilities the animals will have. If the selection criteria is more meat on the breast of a turkey, then the operational breeding procedures will focus on specific traits and technologies which will result in the desired trait. USDA poultry scientist, H.S. Siegel explains the procedure of genetic selection as follows:

> To understand the relationship of the domestic animal to its environment, it is necessary to consider the influence of domestication on the animal character. When animals are first domesticated from the natural state, artificial selection favours those individuals that survive catching, handling, and transport. Selection pressure produces individuals that easily accommodate to the new environment, and characteristics that are genetically associated with nervousness or aggressiveness – characteristics more adaptive to the natural state – tend to be suppressed. In this sense domestication can be viewed as a process of genetic adaptation by artificial selection that emphasizes **traits that are useful or pleasurable to the domesticator.** Because we only measure traits that we can observe or those in which we are interested for productive purposes, there remains some unidentified adaptive variability. The observed average adaptation of the individuals making up a species is therefore less than species adaptation, and this difference is a potential source of variation available for artificial selection. (Emphasis added.)

It is clear that breeding criteria helps advance the structure of intensive animal agriculture and its adverse impacts on the human environment. USDA admissions on the context and criteria of its breeding programs including the use of genetic engineering to produce larger livestock takes on enormous significance.

In response to a lawsuit filed by the FET against the USDA, the latter admits that:

The objective of the Department's research in animal productivity ..., particularly its selective breeding and genetic
breeding research, is to identify and/or develop breeds,
lines, or strains of animals that possess the genetic comple-
ment to ensure efficient production of animal products
under different sets of feed resource situations and different management systems. ...

**Improved livestock that may be developed as a result of
current research in transferring genetic material will be
treated no differently in terms of production systems
from other livestock.** (Emphasis added.)

In short, USDA admits that the context of most of its existing
breeding programs, including its use of genetic engineering in
its breeding program, is the existing structure of intensive
animal agriculture which, as we have seen in detail, has numer-
ous adverse effects on the human environment. This context
will determine the operating criteria of its breeding activities.

This is a very important admission. The criteria embedded in its
breeding programs are criteria which will continue to select
breeds of animals which will thrive under intensive animal
production conditions.

This program approach is evident in the description of goals
and methods that animal scientists in the Agriculture Research
Service of USDA (USDA-ARS) give of their research programs.
Take the example of the position description of Henry Marks,
leader of USDA-ARS's Southern Regional Breeding Project.
Part of his research involves the 'selection for high and low
serum cholesterol responses following ... stress'. This, obviously, is a breeding program designed for poultry reared under
the stressful conditions of intensive production methods.

Another example is the position description of Larry Cundiff, Research Leader of the Genetics and Breeding Research Unit at the Roman L. Hruska US Meat Animal Research Center, Clay Center, Nebraska. The goal of Dr Cundiff's unit is to 'develop systems of mating and selection procedures which ... would increase efficiency of beef, sheep or swine production system'. Dr Cundiff's job includes 'providing information to the beef cattle industry to aid breeders in selection of breeds, systems of crossbreeding, and criterion and procedures of selection to increase efficiency of beef production'.

The Brinster experiment which is being supported by USDA and being closely watched by the biotechnology industry must be viewed in this context. Ralph Brinster, a scientist at the University of Pennsylvania, managed to breed mice the size of rats by combining human growth hormone genes into the genome of mice. Dr Brinster and other scientists hope to duplicate this procedure with livestock to increase the yields of animal production systems.

Now, this transgenic approach to breeding is being done in the context of an animal production industry that is intensifying at a dramatic rate. And so will other genetic engineering experimentations.

One-sided productivity breeding problems are aggravated and worsened because of the existence of biotechnologies and industry capacities to rapidly propagate the desired genetic traits. Hence the results of even a small breeding program involving small numbers of animals can have a tremendous effect on the animal industry.

Take the case of the Holstein breed of dairy cattle. This breed has a genome system which makes it superior to other dairy cattle in terms of whole-milk production per cow. Because this trait was commercially desirable, it rapidly dominated the US dairy industry, accounting for 79% of all US dairy cattle registration and 90% of all US milk production. This rapid dissemination of the genes of this breed is made possible by the creation of reproductive biotechnogies which make swift replication of desired genetic traits feasible.

> ...(G)enetic improvement programs in dairy cattle are heavily dependent upon artificial insemination and progeny testing, which results in a strong relationship between population size and rate of genetic improvement. Artificial insemination reduces the number of sires per breed, especially in the declining minor dairy breeds. The increasing use of embryo transfer also reduces the effective number of female breeders.

The fruits of research and development of biotechnology will ultimately be channelled into and applied in the dominant intensive structure of animal agriculture. This is the meaning of USDA's statement that the improved livestock that may result in transgenetic experiments 'will be treated no differently in terms of production systems from other livestock'. This and similar experimentation by the biotechnology industry will only fuel the adverse impacts that are currently plaguing the intensive production of animal food.

CHAPTER 5

Biotechnology's Impact on Other Areas of Agriculture

What we have seen as adverse impacts of biotechnology in the livestock industry can also be expected for other areas of agriculture. It would therefore be useful to have a brief overview of the current impacts of modern agriculture on resources and the environment.

Contemporary chemical and capital-intensive farming has yielded generous amounts of animal and plant food products in the past four decades. However, major environmental and social disruptions threaten its continued productivity and sustainability.

● The United States has already lost one-third of its topsoil in the last 200 years. In some areas, soil erosion rates are worse than those occurring during the height of the 'dust bowl years' of the 1930s. Soil erosion loss is beyond the critical level of 5 tons per acre per year in more than 112 million acres. Soil erosion in other countries is equally alarming and devastating.

● Toxic chemicals, widely used to attain present yield levels, are starting to kill wildlife, poison the drinking water wells of communities, contaminate the human food chain, and poison thousands of people every year. Through the use of pesticides, industrialized and developing countries are co-participants in energizing a 'circle of poison' which increasingly contaminates the biosphere.

In the United States, 45,000 individuals are poisoned each year. In developing countries, approximately 500,000 people are poisoned annually as a result of rampant use of pesticides.

● Farming with few selected species of plants makes thousands of acres of crops vulnerable to sudden collapse due to uncontrollable outbreaks of pests and diseases.

One of the classic examples is the rapid destruction of thousands of acres of corn worth hundreds of millions of dollars by *Helminthosporium maydis*. In the early 1970s, this virulent strain of fungus broke through the genetic defenses of plants and the pesticide barrier of man and wiped out 710 million bushels of corn, 15% of total US production of this crop.

● The highly publicized prodigious yields of modern agriculture are being obtained at the expense of food quality.

Modern agriculture, especially the use of chemical fertilizers and pesticides affect food quality in two ways. It alters the physiological processes of crop plants making them more susceptible to pest infestations. The use of herbicides in corn, for example, resulted in an increase of corn borer and aphid infestation. The use of toxic chemicals in turn contaminates the food chain. In addition, the extensive use of chemicals also reduces food quality by increasing the quantity of undesirable nitrogenous compounds and altering the specific nutritional characteristics of the species in question. For example, the increased yields of potatoes due to intensive use of chemical fertilizers reduced the true protein content of potatoes and resulted in the rapid deterioration and significant loss of potatoes in storage.

● In addition, modern agriculture, intensive in capital and energy, is vulnerable to currency fluctuations and changes in oil prices. It has been estimated that the supply of fossil fuels will run out in 13 years if all the nations of the world used the planet's oil reserves with the same intensity as the American food system.

Even the Joint Food and Agriculture Council (JFAC), an institution established by the US Congress to help charter the future direction of US agriculture, has acknowledged the many adverse effects of modern agriculture. In addition, the JFAC has advised food policy experts on the highest levels, including the Secretary of the USDA, to expand the concept of agricultural productivity to encompass *total* productivity and a consideration of the environmental and social impact of modern agricultural technologies.

The advent of genetic engineering promises to accelerate these life-threatening environmental impacts of modern agriculture. Just like its impact on animal husbandry, the new biotechnologies promise to accelerate the depletion of the earth's resources and continue the rape of the earth.

Biotechnology engineers are not asking any new questions. They aspire towards the same goals and objectives as did their predecessors who designed chemical and green revolution agriculture. The only difference is one of power and scope. Biotechnology engineers have newer and more powerful tools capable of tampering with all living processes in the biosphere.

However, because biotechnologists are capable of disturbing the natural process in more powerful ways, they will most likely generate new forms of environmental dislocations. Jeremy Rifkin captures the inherent unpredictable dangers of biotechnology:

Genetically engineered products differ from petro-chemical products in several important ways. Because they are alive, genetically engineered products are inherently more unpredictable than petro-chemicals in the way they interact with other living things in the environment. Consequently, it is much more difficult to assess all of the potential impacts that a biotechnical product might have on the earth's ecosystems.

Genetically engineere products also reproduce. They grow and they migrate. Unlike petro-chemical products, it is impossible to constrain them within a given geographical locale. Finally, once released, it is virtually impossible to recall living products back to the laboratory, especially those products that are microscopic in nature. For all these reasons, genetically engineered products pose far greater long-term potential risks to the environment than petro-chemical substances.

PART III

Biotechnology Revolution in Agriculture: Social, Political and Ethical Impacts

CHAPTER 6

Social and Political Impacts of Biotechnology in Agriculture

A similar logic applies in trying to assess the social impacts of biotechnology on human society. Because there has been no fundamental shift in the values and assumptions of those individuals and institutions who hold the resources and power to create the new biotechnologies, one can expect the acceleration of the adverse social impacts that have been experienced with the introduction of the Green Revolution in the rice paddies and crop lands of farmers in the Third World. In addition, there are other dangerous trends unique to the nature of agricultural biotechnology.

Designers of the Green Revolution claimed a 'scale neutrality' for their technology. Because the new seeds and chemicals were divisible into smaller and smaller units and could be aggregated into larger and larger amounts, proponents of the Green Revolution argued that there would be little impact by the new agricultural technologies on the social structure and processes governing the rural areas of the world.

However, as is well-known, the Green Revolution faltered in the mid-seventies as a result of social (and environmental) externalities generated by the packet of inputs and practices associated with the introduction of high yielding varieties (HYVs). Self-sufficient agriculture practised by millions of peasants around the world was dissolved in a manner similar to the way millions of family farmers in industrialized countries were forced out of their farms due to technological advances in farming. Green Revolution discriminated against the landless and poor landowners because its capital-intensive nature required the infusion of financing and other forms of support. The larger and more literate landowners benefitted most from the new technologies. The Green Revolution as a 'technological fix' postponed coming to grips with the complex issues associated with problems in the rural areas including land reform. In some instances, the Green Revolution became a substitute for land reform in terms of increasing food production.

In addition, because the interests of ruling elites were ultimately reflected in the creation of the technology, Green Revolution agriculture focussed narrowly on a few commodity crops. Crops mostly utilized by poor peasants were neglected. Furthermore, the new technology required the use of relatively fertile land for its successful implementation. Ultimately, this led to the technology benefitting only a narrow sector of rural society and aggravated already inequitable patterns of power and resource relationships. Only those with adequate access to credit and wealth became the beneficiaries of these technologies. Income disparities were aggravated leading to discontent and, ultimately, in some countries, to armed insurgency. Those marginal farmers and tenant sharecroppers who had to abandon their farms migrated to the urban areas which were already congested and experiencing its own share of seemingly unresolvable problems.

Green Revolution technology also made developing countries more dependent on industrialized countries both in terms of the science and the inputs required to make this high tech form of agriculture function. This development introduced many new forms of economic, political, and cultural dependencies which threatened self-reliant policies in developing countries.

Green Revolution technologies also operate as *de facto* legislation in both industrialized and developing countries.

Agricultural technologies alter fundamental power relationships and social arrangements between the different political, economic, and cultural groups in society. In this sense, this power of a technology is similar to that enacted by a legislative body. Often because this political dimension of agricultural technology is not perceived, its legislative effects are almost always passed without discussion and deliberation, processes fundamental to democratic rule. Viewed in this context, one can say that unexamined Green Revolution technologies are undermining the democratic process in the countryside by being introduced without hearings and public discussion on its stated goals and implicit effects.

The social problems generated by the Green Revolution continue today. The advent of biotechnology will worsen these problems and create new ones. The creators of the new biotechnologies have not learned from the past. Like their predecessors, they do not design their genetically engineered crops and livestocks with social justice and environmental criteria in mind. Their new technological creations are a step back to the time when the single factor approach reigned supreme. In the process, they are also arresting the learning process that is taking place in some of the public institutions of research responsible for the Green Revolution. Some of these Green Revolution scientists have learned from their mistakes and are trying to introduce, however primitively, a holistic perspective or total productivity criteria in their research agendas. The new biotechnologist believes that the magic of the gene will automatically bring benefits irrespective of social context.

The first signs on the horizon are ominous. Chemical and pharmaceutical companies are stepping up their purchase of seed companies. Shell Co of Netherlands and England, for example, have bought International Plant Breeders (UK), Comanie General de Semillas (Spain), Rothwell Group (UK), Interseeds (Netherlands), IPB (Japan), Nickerson P. Gmbh (West Germany), and North American Plant Breeders (US). Ciba-Geigy of Switzerland has purchased Funk Seeds International (US), Stewart (Canada), and Louisiana Seeds (US).

This consolidation of seed companies with chemical companies breeds a conflict of interest which has the propensity of working against farmers. In the US alone, there are no less than 30 biotechnology companies that are trying to breed new crops that can grow in fields laced with herbicides. In several instances, the company that is genetically engineering this new crop is financially controlled by a parent chemical company like Monsanto. Therefore the new generation of biotechnology crops will be similar to the ones bred for the Green Revolution. The crops will still be dependent on herbicide. What is new, however, is that the genetically altered crops will be specifically suited to the brand of herbicide being produced by the parent chemical company. The trend towards plant patents and breeders rights have only fueled this trend towards control and consolidation.

It is clear that the new biotechnologies are not aimed at making farmers in rural areas develop self-supporting and sustainable agricultural systems. If external control of the agricultural production processes dominated the Green Revolution in the past, the new biorevolution in agriculture will similarly be characterized by new and stronger forms of dominance and manipulation.

The increasingly private nature of the new biotechnologies also supports this trend of undermining community concerns and replacing them with private, unscrutinable agendas. More and more companies are developing in-house capabilities for research in the life sciences. In the past, they have depended on external sources of research and development, mostly by public institutions. Monsanto for example has already invested $40 million in agriculture research and is building a $150 million life science complex. Similarly, Dupont company has funnelled $85 million of research money into the life sciences and genetic engineering and has announced plans for a $300 million research institute for the life sciences.

In addition, the biotechnology industry has also established contracts with leading private universities to do research on molecular biology and various forms of biotechnology. Monsanto, for example, has given over $50 million of research money to Harvard, Washington, and Rockfeller Universities. Hoechst, the giant German chemical company, has given Massachusetts General Hospital $70 million to do research in genetics. Often times, these contracts have stipulations on confidentiality of information. This prevents the free flow of information within the scientific community, a process that is seen as vital to the health of the scientific process.

Furthermore, the marriage between the university and business interests has taken another form. Hidden stock options, directorships in corporate boards, and consulting contracts are currently cementing relationships between academia and businesses. More than 291 such ties exist in universities throughout the United States. For example, Calgene Inc., a biotechnology company based in California, has 16 prominent university scientists as advisers and consultants. Similarly, two-thirds of scientists with industry ties reviewed grant proposals for the National Science Foundation, a prestigious institution which helps determine the direction of basic research in the United States. In addition, nearly one-quarter of the biotechnology related sections at the National Academy of Science, another premier US scientific institution, were occupied by academic scientists with ties to the industry.

The priority setting and peer review processes of the scientific community are seriously threatened by these tenured business-men in academic clothing. Plagued by these conflicts of inter-ests, it is hard to envision that the traditional scientific institu-tions can remain impartial arbitrators in helping resolve the urgent social, ethical, and environmental issues that are arising with the industrialization and rationalization of biotechnology.

The increased privatization of biotechnology brings the spectre of greater control of the whole biotechnological revolution in the hands of a few. Unlike public institutions, there is practi-cally no structure for making these large corporations account-able for their deeds. This issue of control is doubly urgent since biotechnology promises to revolutionize even the most mar-ginal areas of the world – a feat that was difficult to achieve with the traditional Green Revolution methodology. In addition, biotechnology also holds the promise of altering **all** plants and animals, not only a relatively few crops and livestock as was the case with the Green Revolution.

But perhaps the most ominous impact of biotechnology on the social fabric of society is its potential capability of reducing all of agriculture into an automated and controlled industrial process. Through recombinant DNA technology, genetic engi-neers are now increasingly able to transfer one genetic trait from one species to another. They can splice the gene for an essential amino acid and transfer it to the genetic system of a simple organism including bacteria. They, in turn, breed this bacteria with the new genes into billions of similar bacteria. They harvest the bacteria and extract the new amino acids that it contains and use it for nutrition. By scaling up this process, they will be able to produce thousands of tons of this amino acid through industrial processing instead of agricultural production. Because they can control environmental conditions, biotechnologists can automatically schedule the production of desired compounds without having to deal with the uncertainties of weather and labor conditions, a risk which underlies conventional agriculture.

In theory, they can accomplish the same feat with practically all the identified chemical compounds vital to animal and human nutrition as well as organic compounds important to industry.

When biotechnology moves into this direction, the results will be catastrophic. It will require the creation of new social structures, which do not currently exist, to understand, anticipate, and deal with the massive dislocations which are bound to occur.

The recent displacement of agricultural sugar in the world market with fructose produced through biotechnology is a bitter warning to all nations of the power of this new technology. The Philippines and other sugar producing countries are currently suffering tremendous social dislocations as a result of drop of world market prices for sugar. Cane sugar is increasingly being displaced by sugar substitutes produced through a form of biotechnology, immobilized enzyme technology. Due to the resulting negative economics, many conventional sugar factories in developing countries have shut down. Tens of thousands of workers are unemployed. Future developments will not improve the situation. It was estimated that by the mid-1980s, high-fructose corn sweetener captured 10% of the world market and as much as 45% of the US sweetener market.

When food production starts taking place in factories instead of farms, massive unemployment will also result. And, in a market economy, when there is no employment, hunger and starvation cannot be far behind since currency is needed to purchase food. Industrialized and automated food factories obviously will employ only very few workers – a very terrible situation for developing countries where more than 70% of the people reside and work in the countryside.

CHAPTER 7

Ideological and Ethical Impacts of Biotechnology in Agriculture

Towards a Culture of One-Sided Efficiency and 'Death'

Recalling our initial discussion on the three dimensions of technology, we would expect to find that biotechnology also has impacts on the ideological and ethical domains. In the discussions of the environmental and social impacts of biotechnology, I have drawn out the connection between styles of thought and values and the role they play in the creation of the technologies unleashed into the world. It is now necessary to treat this relatively invisible and often incomprehensible level of technology if we are to understand the long-term forces that ultimately give rise to the adverse environmental and social impacts that we have just presented in detail above.

Modern science and technology have an implicit worldview. They operate with a hidden inner logic. Built-in values and ideologies inform their pursuit and application. To understand this, we need to briefly explore the historical roots of modern science and technology.

When Rene Descartes, the father of modern philosophy, formalized the banishment of mind from matter, he gave birth to the methodology of a new science of nature which laid the foundation for the 'scientific revolution'. All qualities which could not be quantified were excluded from scientific consideration. Matter was to be investigated by a strict empiricism. Mind was relegated to the subjective realm of rationalism, which, since then, has had problematic access to the realm of sense perceptible phenomena.

This new methodological principle developed into a precise knowledge of nature that was unknown in all past strivings for knowledge. It laid the basis for a technological revolution that created the industrialized lifestyle and culture of the West and other countries which have adopted Western values.

By the nineteenth century, motivated by their success in astronomy, physics, mathematics, chemistry and technology, many scientists strove to explain life in terms of the inorganic sciences. Darwin crowned this effort with his theory of natural selection which purported to explain the origin of species and organic diversity in nature. Descartes and others banished God from matter. Darwin and his followers banished God from the realm of organic nature.

The program of Descartes, Darwin and other materialistic philosophers and scientists continue to permeate the biological sciences and the general culture of today. Genes are conceived of having godlike faculties, having created all organic phenomena existing today and being able to create new life forms in nature through basically inorganic principles of chance and probability. The mindset that has created the nuclear bomb is the same mentality which is engineering the germplasm of the planet today. It is the vision of dead nature which informs both of them.

Success is a legitimate experience of human nature. When one experiences a fruitful effort after a long and arduous toil, it is natural to experience elation. Success, however, can create a state of somnambulism. It can have a deadening effect on future creativity. While it rewards emphasis on past deeds which have proven fruitful, it curtails an open-minded approach to new phenomena which may not be explicable on the basis of past experience.

Success also offers an almost irresistible temptation to expand the frontiers of a previous methodology to a new cognitional territory. It is hoped that the same methods will unlock the new mysteries which conceal themselves in enigmatic puzzles. In the process an element, totally alien to the workings of the new domain, is imported into the new territory.

Success of one kind has been the destiny of natural science and the technological marvels it has unleashed for the benefit of humanity. However, the scientific method suited for the study of the inorganic also colonized other disciplines to such an extent that, through these intellectual colonies, modern science and technology has introduced a host of deadening and destructive influences into society.

Biology offers an excellent historical as well as on-going example of how an approach that has proven fruitful for the study of dead, inorganic nature is utilized to study the dynamic, sentient, intelligent, and spiritual realm of living nature and humanity.

With the great triumphs of the inorganic sciences in the nineteenth century, scientists became very confident that living plants, animated, sentient animals, and the spiritual essence of man can be completely explained using the laws of physics and chemistry.

> In a way similar to that in which the steam engine produces motion, the intricate organic complication of energy endowed materials in the animal body produces a sum total

of certain effects, which combined in a unity, are called spirit, soul, thought by us....

The words soul, spirit, thought, feeling, will, life, [however,] do not stand for any real things but only for properties, qualifications, functions of living substance, or results of entities that have their basis in the material forms of existence. [L. Buechner (1824-99)]

.... Energy is not a creative God; no essence of things is detachable from the material basis. It is a quality of matter, inseparable from it, eternally inherent in it. Carbon, hydrogen and oxygen are the powers that split the firmest rock and transform it into fluid processes in which life is generated. Change of matter and form in the individual parts while the fundamental structure remains the same is the mystery of animal life. [J. Moleschott (1822-93)]

The Realities of Living Nature: Beyond the Capacity of the Inorganic Sciences to Comprehend

Living nature, however, consists of a domain much wider and richer than can be captured by the inorganic methods of biotechnology. For example, in the environmental sciences, there is a very useful concept called **ecological amplitude** of a species. This refers to the range of habitats that a species can occupy in nature. *Imperata cylindrica,* for instance, can exist in a wide range of soil fertility and light conditions. The concept of ecological amplitude, reveals something of the inherent nature of life as distinct, even if dependent, on its external environment.

Rudolf Steiner (1861-1925), a scientist and philosopher and founder of a new method of science, captures this inner reality of living organisms.

Before everything else, we must direct our thought to this question: Whence do we derive the content of the general class of which we consider the single organic entity a particular instance? We know perfectly well that the specialization is due to the external influences, but the specialized form itself we must derive from an inner principle. The fact that this specialized form itself has evolved we can explain when we study the environment of the entity. Yet this special form is, none the less, something in and of itself; we find it possessed of certain characteristics. We see what is the essential matter. There comes into relation with the external phenomenal world a certain self-formed content which provides us with what we need in order to deduce these characteristics. In inorganic Nature we become aware of a certain fact and we seek a second fact and a third fact in order to explain this; and the result of the inquiry is that the first seems to us the inevitable consequence of the second. In the organic world this is not the case. Here we need still another factor besides the (external) facts. We must conceive at a deeper level than the influences of external conditions something which does not passively allow itself to be determined by these conditions but actively determines itself under their influence.

But what is this fundamental element? It cannot be anything else than that which appears in the particular in the form of the general. But what always appears in the particular is a definite organism. That basic element is, therefore, an organism in the form of the general: a general form of the organism which includes within itself all particular forms.

This general organism we shall call, after the precedent of Goethe, the type.... The type is not elaborated in all its entirety in any single organism. Only our rationalizing thought is capable of grasping this by abstracting it as a general image out of the phenomenal. The type is thus the idea of the organism; the animality in the animal, the general plant in the specific plants.

Under the term **type** we must not imagine anything fixed.... The type is something entirely 'fluidic' out of which may be derived all separate species and families, which we may consider sub-types, specialized types.... All forms [including the primitive and earlier ones] are the result of the type; the first and equally the last are manifestations of the type. It is this type which we must take as the basis for a true organics, not undertaking simply to deduce the single species of [visible] animals and plants one from another....

[Understanding the type necessitates] a revision of our concept of time.... [A new concept of time] would have to show that the deducing of a later from an earlier is no explanation; that the first in time is not the first in principle. Every derivation must be out of what constitutes the principle, and at most it would be necessary to show what factors were effective in bringing it about that one sort of entity evolved in time before another.

The type plays in the organic world the same role as that of the natural law in the inorganic. (Emphasis added.) As the latter gives us the possibility of recognizing each single occurrence as a member of a greater whole, so the type puts us in position to look upon the single organism as a particular shaping of the primal form....

[In inorganic science] our task is to show that a certain sensible fact can appear so and not otherwise because of the existence of this or that natural law.... In the case of a living entity and its manifestations, the case is different. There our task must be to evolve the single form, which meets us in direct experience, from the type – which we must have apprehended. We must perform a mental process of an entirely different sort. We must not simply set the type as

something finished, like a natural law, over against the
single manifestation.

The living organism, as an expression of the Type, also has
'internal forms', one that can only be apprehended through
cognition. An organism is an integration of many systems,
including genetic, cellular, immunological, physiological, developmental, reproductive, morphological, and behavioral,
that are closely and hierarchically interrelated with each other
in a manner which allows the healthy unfolding of the life
functions of the organisms. Thus the concept of the Type
recognizes that a species is a distinct interrelated organization
of these different systems and its integrity consists in its being
able to unfold without obstruction on any level of its being. A
threat to the integrity of the Type would mean a threat to the
healthy and viable functioning of one or more of these many
realms of structure and function that are holistically integrated
in an organism.

In integrating its internal form, the Type tends to **optimize**
rather than to **maximize**. In the act of expressing itself, the Type
has to balance out the thousands of interrelationships inherent
within it. Overexpression of one trait results in the dimunition
of other traits. Cancer is a maximization of the cell principle
over and against the organism principle. One-sided selection
for maximum production, whether through conventional breeding or genetic engineering, is achieved at the expense of the
reproduction process of the animal. Greater speed of growth
results in the underdevelopment of the bone tissues and results
in lameness of animals. Selecting poultry breeds for top production under intensive animal husbandry methods subjects
these birds to stress and induces the formation of fatty tissues at
the expense of bone development.

The implications of this difference between the reality of the inorganic and organic are staggering. Those facts of biology which yield themselves up to the methodology of inorganic nature are really those elements of living nature that are on the verge of death or have died so that they have started exhibiting the regularities of the inorganic realm. The so-called molecules of 'life', DNA, can really be more accurately termed the molecules of disenchanted nature. The world of the genes is really not the world of the living. The methods whereby they are extracted and analyzed belie their affinity with the dead facets of nature. The result is that biotechnology including genetic engineering really set up boundaries against the full understanding of life. This is one of the key reasons why it has continued to fail to explain the emergence of the physical form of the organism on the basis of genetic and molecular development.

Given this context it is understandable and extremely instructive to observe the following interchange which took place at one of the cathedrals of science: the Recombinant DNA Advisory Committee (RAC) of the National Institutes of Health (NIH). The mindset which oversees the promulgation of genetic engineering and biotechnologies in the United States is revealed in its true form. **This mindset, it can safely be assumed, is built-in as the inherent logic of biotechnology wherever it is pursued and practised around the world. This mindset will also be imported by developing countries which aspire to establish flourishing biotechnologies in their own estates.**

[Dr Micheal Fox, Scientific Director of the Humane Society of the United States]: We are on the point of turning animals into biological machines.... [Would] modifying animals...[be] ethically and morally acceptable.... (T)he animal's soma will be modified if animals are made into

biological machines; but 'the psyche of the animal, its telos,
its intrinsic nature' will not be affected. In such a situation,
the mind of the animal may be trapped in a totally alien
body.... [I want] RAC to address this issue....

[Dr Maxine Singer, NIH]: The notion that a species has a
telos (a purpose) contravenes everything we know about
biology. A species can have, and may in the past have had
a telos (an end), namely **extinction**. This is the only telos
known to exist.... (Emphasis added.)

This ideology of death which pervades biotechnology has grave
consequences for the living environment and human society.
Everytime we introduce a technique into the life world, a
technique conceived out of a thought process suitable only for
the understanding and furtherance of dead nature, we are
introducing an alien element, nay, an element of death into the
living relationships of the world. We disenchant living nature
and set up a mummified semblance in its place. With techniques, we drain the living element out of nature. We introduce
the forces of death into everything we create using the methods
of inorganic science and its allied techniques. We create an
ethics and culture of death.

Biotechnology is the modern heir of viewing living nature in
this materialistic and reductionist perspective. As such it
suffers from what I call a **methodological blindness** in believ-
ing that it has the only method of understanding living, sentient, and spiritual reality and that this method enables it to
have an objective grasp of reality. In truth, however, genetic
engineers and biotechnologists are capturing only snippets and
pieces of reality. It cannot help but predictably disrupt the
living relationships of nature and the physical foundation for
the expression of the Type which inheres and permeates or-

ganic entities. Adverse effects on the total organism are bound to arise.

The epidemic of 'production diseases' in animal husbandry, as elaborated in detail above, illustrates the tragic consequences of one-sided pursuit of Neo-Darwinian genetic reductionism and failure in the realm of operational technique.

In addition to this built-in methodological bias, biotechnology also has another inherent objective and logic. Biotechnology and the science which informs it is not about the pursuit after truth. It is a conscious attempt to introduce the value of efficiency into the genetic code of the biosphere. Its true mission is not knowledge and true appreciation of Nature. Its animating desire is to obtain total control of the life force.

As such its apparent successes in the field of molecular genetics must be taken as tentative stabs at the real dynamics of life which animate the core of living Nature. Belief that the DNA is the secret of life will only mask future impacts of the technique on natural and human life.

Part IV
Controlling the
Biotechnology Revolution

CHAPTER 8

Legal Activism and Grassroots Opposition

The pioneering effort to control and regulate biotechnology was being carried out by the FET based in Washington DC, USA. FET aims to insure that a responsible set of local, state, and federal statutes are established to regulate the entire biotechnological revolution. It seeks to develop greater public awareness of and participation in the critical issues and decisions surrounding the imminent commercialization of genetic engineering. In addition, the FET aims to encourage the exploration and development of alternative and sustainable approaches to urgent human needs including food production and health care.

FET's major strategy has been to force review of US agency decisions through litigation before the federal courts. Even though FET is a tiny organization with an annual budget of less than $200,000 in 1985, it has succeeded in halting potentially harmful genetic engineering projects and spawning widespread discussion and debate in many levels of society.

For example, in June 1983, the NIH authorized the first set of experiments involving the deliberate release of genetically modified organisms into the open environment. The NIH approved an experiment which was designed to test the efficacy of genetic engineering in helping prevent frost damage to agricultural crops. This is the famous ice-minus *Pseudomonas syringae* bacteria experiment briefly mentioned in Chapter 1.

In September 1983, FET brought a suit in the US federal court challenging the NIH authorizations. The suit charged that the NIH failed to comply with the National Environmental Policy Act (NEPA). This act requires that whenever a government agency authorizes the release of a new or modified substance into the environment, it must first undertake an environmental assessment study (EA) and/or prepare an environmental impact statement (EIS). In the case of the deliberate release experiments, the government failed to do either.

In this lawsuit, the FET further alleged that the NIH lacked the necessary scientific expertise to judge the potential risk to the environment in conducting these experiments. The official review committee of the NIH lacked representation from the environmental sciences – ecologists, entomologists, plant pathologists, botanists, population geneticists, etc. – and, therefore, could not properly judge the impact of these various experiments on the environment.

The FET also charged that the government failed to develop a set of scientific protocols and a methodology by which to judge the potential risks of releasing genetically modified organisms into the biosphere.

In May 1984, Judge John Sirica of the US District Court for the District of Columbia granted the FET broad relief by prohibiting any deliberate release experiments in the US pending a hearing on the full merits of the case.

This landmark case has received voluminous international coverage and is setting many precedents in regard to environmental regulation of the emerging revolution in genetic engineering.

Since then, the FET has continued to use the courts and the judicial process to oversee the many developments in the area of biotechnology.

For another example, FET's concern for the social and environmental impact of genetically engineered biological weapons motivated it to file a suit against the US Department of Defense (DOD). The objective of the November 1984 suit was to halt the construction of a biological warfare facility at Dugway Proving Grounds in the state of Utah. Through this litigation, FET also wanted to focus public scrutiny on the use of genetic engineering for biological warfare as well as to make this an issue for international discussion and debate.

In May 1985, the federal court granted FET a major first round victory by issuing a permanent injunction against the construction of DOD's bio-warfare facility at Dugway. Through the court victory, the DOD was forced to prepare an environmental impact statement on its Dugway lab.

In addition to these two major victories, FET has successfully challenged and shaped the biotechnology decisions of major US government agencies including USDA, Environmental Protection Agency (EPA), and the White House Office of Science and Technology.

Extra-Legal Activism: Grassroots Opposition

At least three biotechnology experiments had been held up in the United States as a result of local organizing and opposition.

The first experiment to be held up by local opposition was the ice-minus bacteria experiment of Advanced Genetics Sciences

(AGS) in California. Local grassroots activists convinced the County Board of Supervisors in Monterey, California, site of the AGS experiment, to declare a 45-day moratorium on all releases of genetically altered organisms in the country.

The second experiment to be stopped by local opposition was Monsanto's planned release of a genetically engineered microbial pesticide. Monsanto transferred the pesticidal gene of *Bacillus thuringensis* to a soil bacteria, *Pseudomonas flourescens*. Through this procedure, Monsanto had hoped to treat corn seeds with their genetically engineered microbial pesticide and protect corn crops from cut worms.

Local citizens were alarmed by the experiments and started organizing against the experiment. A resolution by the city of St Charles, Missouri, near the site of the Monsanto experiment, expressed concern about the experiment. This concern was fuelled by the discovery that there were some unresolved safety questions with the Monsanto product. In the meantime, the EPA, which was reviewing the product, was pressured with the threat of a court suit by the FET not to approve the product until all the safety questions had been answered. In the end, the EPA instructed Monsanto to conduct further studies on its product. In frustration, Monsanto withdrew its application for the microbial pesticide produced through genetic engineering.

The third experiment stopped by local opposition was an attempt in 1986 by Dr Steven Lindow from the University of California to release his genetically altered ice-minus bacteria into the environment. This was the same bacteria that a few years earlier was stopped by the FET. Californians from several countries teamed up to put a halt to the experiment. Because of their widely publicized opposition, the University of California voluntarily postponed the tests pending further studies on the environmental impact of the bacteria.

CHAPTER 9

Sustainable Agriculture: An Alternative to Biotechnology

Opposition, whether through the courts or through local organizing, is crucial and important. However, opposition is a stopgap measure and by itself, will not stem the tide of the coming biotechnological revolution. Human needs including food and human development have to be met. And in the end, if there are no alternative ways of meeting these needs, any technology, including biotechnology, will be used no matter what the consequences are.

In this sense, the pursuit of more sustainable forms of agriculture is of central importance in meeting the challenge of biotechnology. Do we grow our crops with genetically engineered resistance to polluting herbicides or do we develop ecological forms of agriculture which work with the rhythms and cycles of nature to achieve the same end of feeding humanity?

Proven alternatives to conventional agriculture exist in many parts of the world. Documentation during the past decade has shown that these scientific alternative agricultural technologies are productive, economical, resource-conserving, and appropriate to many farming situations in both industrialized and developing countries.

For example, one long-term study done by a team of scientists from Washington University at St Louis showed that alternative agriculturists, using only 40% the energy, made as much net income as conventional farmers. These alternative farmers also suffered less erosion damage than the conventional farmers. A 1980 study by the USDA concluded that the soil and crop management practices of alternative agriculturists 'are also those which have been cited as best management practice (from the viewpoint of government standards) for controlling soil erosion, minimizing water pollution, and conserving energy'. The USDA study team also 'strongly' felt that research and education programs for alternative agriculture be pursued for their 'potential benefits to agriculture both at home and abroad'.

The governments of France, Germany, Switzerland, and the Netherlands have all undertaken comprehensive studies on alternative agriculture. Their finds were favourable and recommendations made to continue further studies and support of alternative agriculture.

All over the world, many conferences have been held and organizations formed to pursue alternative agriculture. There are at least two organizations trying to encourage the development of sustainable agriculture on a global basis: the International Federation of Organic Agriculture Movements and the International Alliance for Sustainable Agriculture.

The Enormous Potential of and Support for Sustainable Agriculture

An increasing number of individuals and institutions, estimated to number in the millions, are either exploring alternative agricultural practices or supporting initiatives that help establish viable alternatives to the present system of farming. They envision a sustainable agriculture – farming systems that are environmentally sound, economically viable, socially just, and humane.

In the US alone, 11.4 million households are interested in organic gardening methods. And out of 38 million gardening households, 36 million used 'organic' nutrient sources in addition to commercial fertilizers. The Rodale Press publications including *Organic Gardening* and *Prevention* reach 12 million people. There are also more than 6,500 health food stores servicing tens of thousands of consumers who seek natural foods. The millions of adherents to environmentalism and appropriate technology are natural allies of alternative agriculturists. Many of the 37.5 million 'inner-directeds', as defined by Stanford Research Institute (SRI) International, have values and existential guidelines which can blend harmoniously with a good segment of the sustainable agriculture movement.

There are many sustainable and viable alternatives to present commercial farming. They are known by many names including organic farming, eco-agriculture, biological farming, natural farming, Bio-Dynamic agriculture, indigenous farming system, permaculture, and agroecosystems. For an overview of organic farming in the United States, see *Report and Recommendations on Organic Farming* by the USDA. For a more thorough and substantive overview of sustainable agriculture systems, see the Dutch government report on alternative agriculture published as a special issue of the journal, *Agriculture and Environment*, Volume 5, Numbers 1 & 2, March 1980.

The Bio-Dynamic/French Intensive Method of Food Production: Its Relevance to Food Production in Developing Countries

Of immense potential significance for developing countries and small scale agriculture in industrialized countries is the Bio-Dynamic/French Intensive (BD/FI) Method of food production.

Alan Chadwick, a master horticulturist from England, combined the proven practices of Bio-Dynamic farming with the established horticultural techniques of French truck farmers to produce what is now known worldwide as the Bio-Dynamic/French Intensive Method. Since the early days at the University of California at Santa Cruz until his death in 1980, Alan Chadwick influenced the lives of thousands of individuals. Continued dissemination of his ideas by leading practitioners has now exposed hundreds of thousands of individuals and institutions into a consideration of the potential and promise of the BD/FI Method for agriculture in developed and developing countries. Over 250,000 people in 50 countries are now using variations of this method.

What are the potentials of the BD/FI Method?

Studies done by the University of California-Berkeley at Ecology Action in California have established the tremendous capacity of the BD/FI Method to regenerate worn-out and marginal soils. The studies have shown that 12 inches of precious, fertile topsoil can be produced in a few years by this biointensive method in contrast to the natural process of soil formation that takes hundreds of years to produce the same quantity and quality of top-soil.

The original soil base of the experiment was a highly compacted, cement-like parking lot. A few years of double digging and other cultural practices including composting, intercropping, and avoidance of toxic chemicals, have converted this parking lot into one of the most fertile and productive land surfaces in America.

It is, therefore, not surprising to discover that yields produced by this transformed soil were four times the national average for mechanized vegetable farming. Furthermore, these incredibly high yields were attained with only one-third to 1/31st the water requirements, half to no purchased organic nitrogen fertilizer, 1/100th the energy used, and no soil erosion as contrasted to conventional methods of producing vegetables. A balanced diet for seven to 30 vegetarians can be produced on a half acre piece of land. **All these can be accomplished without resorting to biotechnology.**

This method clearly holds the potential of producing generous amounts of food from marginal soils with a minimum of capital and fossil fuel inputs.

It is important to note that the Chadwick method is only one variation of the Bio-Dynamic Method of farming. In addition to the fruits, vegetables, flowers, herbs, and landscape plants that are grown using Chadwick's approach, a full range of crops and livestock can be grown and raised using the Bio-Dynamic Method. In Australia, for example, the Bio-Dynamic Method has proven itself practical and successful in producing a full range of crops including wheat, rice, pasture, sugarcane and a range of tropical fruits. Currently, one million acres in Australia are managed by 4,000 farmers using the Bio-Dynamic Method. In addition, thousands of acres are farmed altogether in the United States and Europe using the Bio-Dynamic Method.

To understand the tremendous potential of the BD/FI Method for Third World agriculture, it is important to quickly enumerate environmental and social conditions which predominate in developing countries.

In developing countries, most of the people reside in the rural areas. In both countryside and cities, the population density is high. The birth rates are explosive. Majority are poor and malnourished. Many do not have access to financial and capital resources. Most peasants are unemployed and politically marginal. Among those who are lucky to have a piece of land, the sizes of acreage are small. Sophisticated indigenous agricultural knowledge is ignored.

Agriculture in the Third World has to be cognizant of the differing ecological traits of tropical ecosystems. For example, nutrient storage in the tropics is located more in living and dead biomass than in the inorganic components of the soil system. Species diversity is also more prevalent in tropical ecosystems in comparison to those in the temperate regions of the world.

The BD/FI agriculture, introduced into this setting, has many advantages.

It is biologically more appropriate to tropical ecosystems than conventional farming methods which rely on external control of biological systems through heavy usage of chemicals and equipment. Marginal tropical soils are highly leached and characterized by low nutrient reserves (depressed cation exchange capacity) and minimal microbial activity. Crop response to chemical fertilizers under these conditions are minimal or practically nil. The BD/FI Method systematically builds up soil fertility and increases crop productivity.

The BD/FI Method also holds more potential for interacting appropriately with existing traditional methods of agriculture. Like indigenous farming systems, the BD/FI Method recycles organic wastes, uses simple tools, relies on a minimum of external inputs, integrates animals into the cropping system, practices crop diversity, regulates pests through internal agroecosystems processes including predation. Unlike modern chemical farming, BD/FI agriculture respects traditional agriculture and tries to develop from and build upon indigenous farming techniques.

Third World agriculture is characterized by small, subsistence, and impoverished farming operations. Unemployment is rampant in both rural and urban areas. On the national level, many countries have balance of payments and foreign exchange problems. The BD/FI Method is ideal under such circumstances because it can be started with very small acreages (even as small as 1,000 square feet) and does not require inordinate amounts of capital to establish an economically viable operation. In addition, because it is labour intensive, it offers one answer to unemployment. On the national level and long-term perspective, it can allow developing countries to be self-reliant on food and impervious to the fluctuations and hazards of the world market for farm products and materials.

In addition to being a source of economic livelihood, the BD/FI Method can also be designed to be used in nutritional programs for the urban and rural poor. For example, squatter communities in many urban areas of the world can be aided by establishment of horticultural parks which can enhance the level of nutrition of many malnourished children and adults. Furthermore, because the BD/FI Method does not utilize toxic chemicals, the quality of the food produced is also improved.

The BD/FI Method is also environmentally sound. Ecosystems are conserved instead of destroyed. Bio-intensive farms can also become the focal points for the rediscovery and conservation of native plants and animals adapted to specific sites. These BD/FI initiatives can then become local, decentralized, peasant-controlled gene banks in the form of small agroecosystems which utilize indigenous species.

It must be emphasized that the BD/FI Method is only one among many possible approaches to sustainable agriculture in the developing countries. Other farming systems including agro-forestry or multi-storied agroecosystems are appropriate for farming conditions in the Third World.

The BD/FI Method is not a panacea for all agricultural problems. However, judicious application of the BD/FI Method under appropriate social, climatic, and soil conditions can prove highly beneficial and helpful to individuals and their communities.

The Need to Promote Sustainable Agriculture

Alternative agriculture is a sleeping giant. It slumbers because, among others, it has no awareness and vision of its tremendous size and power. It has not pulled itself together.

Awakened, however, this giant will reshape the international agricultural landscape. Awakened, there is no doubt that it will gradually and beneficially replace and/or transform conventional agricultural systems as the major mode of sustainable food production for the planet.

But, today, the reality is that this massive potential remains unmanifested. Although there are more than 30,000 alternative farms in the US, they make up less than 1% of the total population of farms. Although there are thousands of acres being farmed alternatively in Europe, these again are less than 1% of total farming acreage. Although many small centers for alternative agriculture exist in the Third World, these are a drop in the ocean of Green Revolution agriculture which continues to be aggressively promoted. Hundreds of appropriate indigenous farming systems are being wiped out in the process including the thousands of local varieties that house the biological diversity of the planet.

I have intentionally belaboured this point on the need to pursue sustainable agriculture with a reason. As a global community, we are facing a critical juncture. We have two paths to the future. We either pursue an ecological partnership with the living systems of our fragile planet or we assert our total rulership over the forces of nature and totally redesign our living environment through biotechnology. **The moment we forget that we have an alternative to biotechnological intervention in agriculture, then, at that point, we perish with our lack of vision.** But the sooner we move on the track of deep stewardship of the resources of the earth and the sooner we acknowledge our deep indebtedness and relationship with nature, the quicker we create a world of hope and promise. It could even be that there will be facets of biotechnology that we will take with our journey onward. However, it will be one imbedded in the context of an ecological vision and wisdom.

CHAPTER 10

Transforming Modern Science and Technology: The Second Scientific Revolution

Our undertaking to establish sustainable agriculture systems in place of a bioengineered world of artificial nature will be bolstered from a most important source. I refer to the emergence of a new breed of science that is already visible on the horizon.

Earlier, we have seen how the scientific and technological revolution of the last 400 years has given us the vast panorama of physical and social forms that surround us today. They inform every facet of our existence. They have bestowed precious gifts to humanity. But they have also dehumanized us and have wreaked havoc on nature.

In a similar manner, a **new, second and more holistic scientific revolution** is upon us. It is currently reshaping our understanding of the process of knowledge and is resurrecting those real elements of life, sentience, and spirit that have been banished with the advent and dominance of the old scientific revolution. It is reconceptualizing the meaning and goals of scientific and technological activity. Just as the old scientific revolution has shaped our modern civilization, the worldview of the new science will become the staging ground for a new and more reverent partnership with nature and other cultures.

The New Science: A Few Examples of Revolutionary Discoveries

Since this has been a lengthy paper and there is barely room left for a comprehensive treatment, let me just cite a few symptomatic scientific discoveries that have permanently altered the scientific landscape in the last few decades. I will first simply describe the discoveries. In a later section, I will draw out their importance to our discussion on biotechnology.

● The discoveries of the new physics, quantum mechanics, are probably the most well known to the general public due to the publication of such books as the *Tao of Physics* and *The Dancing Wu Li Masters*, among others.

Among the time honored principles that have fallen as a result of the new physics is the old logic which says that, if A = A and B = B, then A cannot be B. This harmless looking equation is the basis of the old scientific revolution's concept of space, here only one object, not two or more, can occupy a certain space.

Now, it is an accepted fact of the new physics that light can be conceived both as a particle and a wave. In effect, the new physics is saying that A and B can both occupy the same space.

The Newtonian concept of time has also been revised with the advent of the new physics. Physicists have discovered that, in a two particle system, the spin of one of the particles simultaneously affects the spin of the other particle without the transfer of energy or matter. 'If the statistical predictions of quantum theory are true, an objective universe is incompatible with the law of local causes.' The experimental demonstration of non-locality indicates that cause-effect relationships can exist between objects that are not physically in touch with each other and may be a few feet or millions of miles away from each other.

● In biology, Weismann's barrier, one of the foundation stones of modern Darwinian theory, is being superceded. Weismann established a doctrine which asserted the independence of the germline from environmental influences. Weismann's work is one of the key theories behind the Neo-Darwinian claim that all influences on behaviour and form of the organism originate from the genes.

However, recent experiments by Chris Cullis at the University of Colorado question the validity of Weismann's barrier. Cullis has developed experimental evidence to show that fertilizers can induce changes in the genetic system of some varieties of flax. These changes are then passed on to the next generation.

Ironically, modern molecular biology has provided one of the strongest arguments against the Neo-Darwinian theory of macro evolution. If the Neo-Darwinian theory is correct, those species that are closest to each other should have very similar genetic properties. However, modern studies in molecular biology have shown that:

> The classification system that is derived from ... compara-
> tive molecular studies is a highly ordered non-overlapping
> system composed entirely of groups within groups, of
> classes which are inclusive or intermediate classes, and
> therefore none of the groups traditionally cited by evolu-
> tionary biologists as intermediate gives even the lightest
> hint of a supposedly transitional character .... Thus, mol-
> ecules, like fossils, have failed to provide the elusive inter-
> mediates so long sought by evolutionary biology .... [In
> contrast, one] of the most remarkable features of these new
> biochemical discoveries is undoubtedly the way in which

the pattern of molecular diversity seems to correspond to
the predictions of typology [elaborated by the great com-
parative anatomists of the nineteenth century].

Recently, Rupert Sheldrake has developed a testable hypothesis regarding the existence of what he calls 'morphogenetic
fields' in nature. In a similar way that the new physics postulates the transfer of information beyond space and time,
Sheldrake's theory postulates that morphogenetic fields can
transmit its influence in a way which is not explainable by
conventional physics and chemistry. Morphogenetic fields are
responsible for the emergence and transmission of form from
one generation to the next generation.

Sheldrake's morphogenetic fields have an uncanny similarity
to the nature of thought. One can experience thought and the
thinking process as being found nowhere in space and time.
Memories of the past and visions that create the future can be
experienced and re-experienced again and again in the present.
Memory is not localized in any specific hemisphere of the brain.

A recent discovery supports Sheldrake's theory of
morphogenetic fields. Radioactive tracer studies have shown
that **all** the molecules of the human body, including the DNA,
are replaced in approximately seven-year cycles. However,
despite the flux of molecules in the human body, the human
form manages to maintain itself. This discovery points to the
existence of an underlying reality presently undiscovered by
modern biology. Molecular biologists are starting to realize that
the genetic code does not contain the instructions for the three-
dimensional shape of protein molecules. This biological anomaly
points to the existence of an 'organizer' which is not the regula-
tor gene but an entity, a totality, a morphogenetic field, if you
will, that operates and manages biological processes in the
organism.

Interestingly enough, both the typological discoveries of molecular biology and Sheldrake's morphogenetic fields support Steiner's concept of the 'type' discussed earlier. Sheldrake's morphogenetic fields also bear striking similarities (although there are differences) with Bio-Dynamic agriculture's concept of a 'formative force' in nature.

● Modern brain research has shown that, contrary to the tenets of materialistic science, consciousness as a reality is both independent from the biophysical mechanisms of the body and exerting control on the neural pathways of the nervous system. Consciousness, of course, depends on the physical brain for its physical manifestation but it has a content of its own distinct from the brain. Nobel Laureate John Eccles, for example, has shown through his studies with the brain's supplementary motor area (SMA) that the mind governs brain activity and the pattern of firing of the brain cells.

This finding is so patently obvious to the common human experience of freedom as to require no experimental verification. However, the ideology of materialistic science has so enslaved the human mind that it has had difficulties shedding the ideological fetters to the human spirit.

● In the study of language, Owen Barfield has discovered a curious aspect of ancient language. The farther one goes back in time, the more the words of ancient language convey both inner and outer meanings.

Take the case of the Greek word, *pneuma*. This word describes both a reality external to the perceiver, that is, the wind. **At the same time,** it also describes an inner process, that is, breath. In addition, it also refers to a transcendent reality, that is, *pneuma* as spirit.

Through a study of such historically verifiable phenomena, Barfield came up with the conclusion that nature including human beings have an 'inside'. In addition Barfield concludes that early humanity had a different consciousness than present day human beings. Early humanity had a 'participatory' awareness – a consciousness that participated with the internal processes of Nature. Modern humanity has an 'onlooker' or detached consciousness, only able to perceive the surfaces of things. Through conscious participation, the next stage in the evolution of consciousness, modern humanity can learn to re-integrate itself with the inner and outer being of nature. Barfield identifies active or poetic imagination as the path towards conscious participation.

The New Science Undermines the Methodological Hegemony and Doctrines of Conventional Science and Biotechnology

The new realities being discovered by the new scientific revolution call into serious question the underlying assumptions and theories of many fields in conventional science including the working hypothesis and ideas of biotechnology.

In contrast to the mechanical concept of living entities as aggregates of DNA, the new science offers the fuller concept of the 'organism'. The different parts of the organism are intimately connected in a web of relationships that are fluid but precisely defined. No part can be maximized at the expense of other parts. One can use chemical fertilizers to increase crude biomass yields, but the nutritional quality of plants suffers. One can breed animals for faster growth rates and earlier maturity but only at the expense of solid bone structure and decreased reproductive performance.

The breakdown of Weismann's barrier also douses the fires of biotechnology with **uncertainty**. Traits are not solely governed by genes. There is no strict one-way causation flowing from the gene to the trait. The trait is an emergent quality, dependent on the environment and other factors in addition to the gene. The potential for hazards awaits the products of biotechnology.

When Descartes banished consciousness and mind from external phenomena, the old science maintained his legacy and dealt only with surfaces and presumed that living beings have no 'inside'. In contrast, the new science envisions animal life as having an inward quality and possessed of sentience and emotions. Therefore, it makes sense to expect that animals bred for and raised in factory farms experience stress which in turn results in illness and loss of productivity. With the new science, Michael Fox's concern about the effect of biotechnology on the *telos* and *eidos* of animals becomes a legitimate scientific question, truly worthy of pursuit.

In place of the literalness of the old science, the new scientific revolution provides documented evidence for the concept of co-inherence: Multiple realities can occupy the same space. Biotechnology discovers only one facet of reality: those amenable to manipulation and control. Other realities of the organism are methodologically ignored. The phenomenon of 'unintended side-effects' of modern technology including biotechnology is the price that modern civilization pays for honoring their one-dimensional god.

The new science restores the common root of mind and nature in the spirit. The new scientists have observed that, in both mind and nature, 'similarity is proximity and form dominates'. Barfield's work is one of the clearest demonstration of this intimate relationship between mind and nature. Archetypal psychologists including James Hillman also lend support to this rather stunning re-discovery. The implications of this discovery for the curative process in medicine and the assessment of the spiritual impacts of biotechnology are going to be part and parcel of the new scientific agenda.

Chapter 11

Conclusion

Every great scientific and technological revolution in history comes packaged in the form of benefits and costs. The more powerful the technology is in promising an immediate economic benefit, the greater becomes the potential for long-term environmental, economic, political, ideological, and ethical dislocations.

The new biotechnologies including genetic engineering provides civilization with the ultimate form of power over the living forces of nature. We now have a technology at our disposal which allows us to begin intervening into the genetic blueprints of life. There are many short term benefits to be derived from this emerging science and technology. However, it would be naive and disingenious to believe that there will be no adverse impact on the environment and on human society.

In the past, governments around the world have narrowly focussed on the question of potential benefits of new scientific and technological breakthroughs, with little or no attention paid to the long term environmental and social costs of new innovations. At the beginning of the nuclear technology revolution and petrochemical revolution, policy and decision makers failed to address the hard questions concerning potential externalities of these technologies. As a result, our generation and our children's generation have been forced to deal with the mounting environmental, economic, and social bill including from nuclear waste dumps, Chernobyl, Bhopal, acid rain, and the pesticidal 'circle of poison'.

Now, with the emergence of the new biotechnology revolution, the promoters of this new technology are once again failing to develop a coherent framework to assure a proper regard for the long-term health of the human and natural environments.

A bold new departure must be taken with regard to the emerging scientific, technological, and social revolutions being spawned by the new biotechnologies. It is time that we force our governments to construct a regulatory procedure that would provide a comprehensive foresight analysis for all decisions regarding the development and commercial application of genetic engineering technology. The environmental, economic, social, and cultural impacts of each new genetically engineered product or program must be scrutinized. It would be inappropriate and irresponsible for any government agency or business corporation to release any genetically engineered product into the environment until such time as the appropriate scientific studies to judge risks and effects have been completed.

We bear a heavy burden and responsibility. We have before us a technology that can utterly change our lives, the lives of our children, and the natural environment in less than two decades. In addition, we are the first generation in human history to have the opportunity to scrutinize this technology in advance of its widespread application and commercialization.

We must not only scrutinize and criticize. We must also launch new initiatives in the field, including sustainable agriculture and holistic health practices, to address the food and health needs that are tempting people to make a Faustian bargain with biotechnology.

We must expand our developmental and environmental activism to address the challenges that this new technology forces upon us. Much will depend on our being awake to the tasks that lie ahead as the dawn of biotechnology gradually extends its mixed influences into all corners of the earth.

List of Abbreviations

AGS	–	Advanced Genetics Sciences
BD/FI	–	Bio-Dynamic/French Intensive Method of agriculture
BgH	–	Bovine growth hormone
BIOTECH	–	Philippine Institute for Biotechnology
Bt	–	*Bacillus thuriengensis*
CADI	–	Center for Alternative Development Initiatives
CAST	–	Council for Agricultural Science and Technology
CDC	–	Centers for Disease Control
DOD	–	Department of Defense, US
EPA	–	Environmental Protection Agency, US
FAO	–	Food and Agriculture Organization
FDA	–	Food and Drug Administration, US
FET	–	Foundation on Economic Trends, US
GAO	–	General Accounting Office, US
GATT	–	General Agreement on Tariffs and Trade
HgH	–	Human growth hormone
HUGO	–	Human Genome Organization, US
HYV	–	High Yielding Variety
IARCS	–	International agriculture research centers
ICs	–	Indigenous communities
IPR	–	Intellectual Property Rights
IRRI	–	International Rich Research Institute, Philippines
JFAC	–	Joint Food and Agriculture Council, US
NEPA	–	National Environment Policy Act, US
NGO	–	Non-Governmental Organization
NIH	–	National Institutes of Health, US
RAC	–	Recombinant DNA Advisory Committee, US
UNDP	–	United Nations Development Program
USAID	–	The United States Agency for International Development
USDA	–	US Department of Agriculture
USDA-ARS	–	Agriculture Research Service of the US Department of Agriculture

N